Courtesy George Roy

# Maud Lewis
## World Without Shadows

Lance Woolaver

T0204212

SPENCER BOOKS
Halifax, Nova Scotia

This book is published by Spencer Books of Halifax, Nova Scotia and published in Canada. Spencer Books is a part of Sisko Holdings Limited, a "Mom and Pop" business with postal address and head office at No. 519, 1472 Martello Street, Halifax, Nova Scotia B3H4K8. Readers are directed to the website of Spencer Books for further information about Maud Lewis and Lance Woolaver and the original stage play *Maud Lewis World Without Shadows*. For further examples of the artworks of Maud Lewis see *The Illuminated Life of Maud Lewis* by Lance Woolaver and Bob Brooks, Nimbus Publishing, Halifax, Nova Scotia, and the children's books *From Ben Loman to the Sea* and *Christmas With the Rural Mail*, Nimbus Publishing. The first complete biography of Maud and Everett Lewis is contained in the Spencer Books publication *Maud Lewis The Heart on the Door*. All are available from your local bookstore and on-line. Spencer Books supports your local bookstore and your public library. The author and publisher appreciate the support of our readers and hope that unauthorized use of these years of work can be stopped. Those who believe in the work of writers will support this hope.

Woolaver, Lance, 1948 –
Maud Lewis World Without Shadows

1.      Lewis, Maud, 1901-1970; Woolaver, Lance, 1948 -.
2.      ND249.L447W66  759.11  C96-950138-2
3.

ISBN 978-0-9950017-1-8


Front cover photo of Maud and Ev courtesy Elsa Hanbury.
Back cover photo of the author courtesy of Bob Brooks.
Book design: Rand Gaynor

# Lance Gerard Woolaver

## Books
The Illuminated Life of Maud Lewis (with Bob Brooks)
Christmas with Maud Lewis (with Bob Brooks)
The Poor Farm
The Outlaw League
The Metal Sparrow
Maud Lewis The Heart on the Door (dedicated to Bob and Marion Brooks)

## Plays
Brindley Town
The Poor Farm
Lord Strange
Maud Lewis - World Without Shadows
Portia White - First You Dream
Evelyn Richardson - The Keeping of Lights
Kenny Paul

## Children's Books
Duck, Duck and Duck
The Humble Mumbles
Christmas with the Rural Mail
From Ben Loman to the Sea
Change of Tide (with Anna Gamble)
Mr. Christmas (with Lee Tanner)
Darwin (with Lee Tanner)

## Libretto
The Heart on the Door

## Songs
The Noel Cantata (Notteroy and Porsgrunn, Norway)

## Filmscripts
The Illuminated Life of Maud Lewis (Documentary)
Maud Lewis - The Heart on the Door (Feature)
The Outlaw League / La Gang des Hors-la-Loi (Feature)
The Noggins (TV half-hour with Ron Foley MacDonald)

## Radio
The Poor Farms (3-part documentary series, CBC Atlantic, with Ron Foley MacDonald)

## Dedication

This play is dedicated to Thornton Wilder. Uncle Teddy Woolaver and I travelled to meet Mr. Wilder in Connecticut in 1968. We were picking apples on a work gang near Worcester, Massachusetts. Mr. Wilder was kind enough to autograph a copy of *Our Town*.

## Productions

Productions of *Maud Lewis WORLD WITHOUT SHADOWS* include full productions by King's Theatre of Annapolis Royal; Neptune Theatre, Halifax, (Linda Moore, Artistic Director); the Blythe Festival of Blyth, Ontario (Eric Coates, Artistic Director; Gil Garratt, Director); Ship's Company Theatre of Parrsboro (Michael Chiasson, Director); and a national broadcast with CBC Radio. The play has held several house records. The playwright would like to thank Bob White of Alberta Theatre Projects, as he then was, for the grace of using the production title "Nova Scotia Theatre Projects" in the first co-op workshop of this play in Halifax. Directors, actors and producers may contact Spencer Books for production rights.

## Cast

These roles have been played by Black, White and Mi'kmaq actors. The cast of the first production at King's Theatre of Annapolis Royal featured Ken Maher, Walter Borden, Phyllis Essex-Fraser, John Nickerson, Donna Holmes and Lucky Campbell. Jeremiah Sparks joined us for the Ship's Company and Neptune productions. Nicola Lipman, the esteemed Canadian actor, has played "Maud" to great artistic and box office success. And only yesterday, I happened to meet Deb Allen, who twice played "Bert" in this play, in the library down the street.

## Maud Lewis

A little and twisted sparrow of a lady. As with Hardy's *Darkling Thrush*, her spirit burns brighter than the day.

## Everett Lewis

Maud's crafty husband. As Night Watchman at the Poor Farm, he walks the wards at night.

## Bert Potter

Maud's friend. A good mother and merchant, Bert sells to the tourist trade the patchwork called a "crazy quilt".

## Big Junior

A Deacon in the African Baptist Church. Jack of all trades, Junior works for both the spiritual and the temporal. He once took, in a game of cards, the pay of his fellow labourers loading pitprops on a German ship. The King James has given him his one last chance.

**The Judge**
Maud's patron. The Judge can trace his literary ancestry to Mark Twain's "Judge Thatcher," Mr. Wilder's "Stage Manager," and most directly Burl Ives' portrait of Tennessee's "Big Daddy."

**Little Juny**
Junior's gifted son. A charismatic and talented child, Juny is sifting through the challenges of youth and County.

Our characters are folk figures. All bring to the Maud Lewis House a simple, singular characteristic. The action, ranging from mild argument to murder, takes place within their memory and argument. As Maud's paintings spark revelations, life in the House and County no longer seems so straightforward. All are ghosts returned for the time it takes to lay their burdens down. Although this work is fiction, all characters began as persons I once knew in Digby. All, alas, with the exception of these evenings, are no longer with us.

**Cuts**
The Director may cut lines at will. I over-write my plays. The Director is free to weave our wandering ghosts into any likely scene. The Director may introduce characters. For example, to save production costs, Juny's mother is an offstage presence. There's no good reason why Pearline can't appear. She certainly casts light on Maud's life and I liked sitting in her kitchen. Maud's daughter, Catherine Dowley, is another life that haunts the story.

We might remember that the home of this play was a divided community of villages and country roads. This division was first explored in Nova Scotia in the Walter Borden production of James Baldwin's *Blues for Mister Charlie*. There were, in those Digby days, Irish Protestants and Irish Catholics, First Nations Mi'kmaq, French-speaking Acadians, African Baptist "Coloureds" and English-speaking "Whites." The bankers, merchants and mariners were mostly Scots, Anglo-Irish and Acadian. The Hessian "Deutsch" were a thin remainder. Families were speaking remnants of old languages. Blends of all these races, languages and religions lived near and by, but not with, one another. The Woolavers arrived in Nova Scotia on the sailing ship *Pearl* in 1751.

**The Time**
Maud did not pass away until 1970, but this play takes place in the 1950's. I know that decade well enough to be comfortable and not enough to be restricted. Readers may wish to borrow the pictorial biography *The Illuminated Life of Maud Lewis* (Nimbus Publishing, Halifax, Nova Scotia, 1995; by Bob Brooks and Lance Woolaver) from their local library. The time and place of this play are pictured within. The first full-length biography of Maud and Everett Lewis, *Maud Lewis*

*THE HEART ON THE DOOR*, has recently been published with Spencer Books, Halifax, Nova Scotia, 2016.

### Music

Companies who find themselves in funds may commission a soundscape. A flat-top Gibson, as Everett places tins beneath the raindrops, would be good. With community theatre, where talent is more plentiful than money, live and acoustic music could be placed within the blackouts and the quiet scenes. A battery-operated radio could play a country tune. Ev was possessed of an old blue Melmac radio powered by T. Eaton batteries. A wind-up record player would work. Maud, as I have written in my books, enjoyed her Edison cylinder player. These devices cast squeaky harmonies to the breezes. Maud loved the songs of Wilf Carter *(Bluebirds on Your Windowsill)* and Jimmie Rodgers (*Rock All Your Babies to Sleep*). I would enjoy the Browns' cover of Piaf's *Les Trois Cloches* (*The Three Bells*). It's the first biography in song I can recall.

### The Set

Our set is the Maud Lewis House, ten feet by twelve, more or less, of shadows and colour. This play was part of the 1996 campaign, as recorded on the front page of the *Globe & Mail*, to get the Maud Lewis House out of a Nova Scotia Lands and Forests shed. The House had rotted for a decade in that shed. Butterflies, flowers, bees and hummingbirds decorate the doors and windows and the stove. Sweet peas spring from windowsill tins. The play begins with two bright windows. At the end we find but one. The stove might best be placed to show Maud's paintings. Maud set her paintings up on the warming oven to dry. Much of the action takes place in Maud's small corner and about and around her decorated window. Apart from the stove, little furniture: sticks of chairs and a table. In Maud's sunny corner: a decorated window and a folding tray for boards and brushes. She never owned a proper easel. Scallop shells and tins hold her paints. She sits to paint in a little rocking chair and rocks quietly as she works. On the door, a heart, as may be seen in my books *The Illuminated Life of Maud Lewis* (with the wonderful Bob Brooks) and *Maud Lewis THE HEART ON THE DOOR*. Swans, black and white, glide on the door. The wallpapers are decorated with Maud's paintings of deer, dogs and sundry fancies. Nails, hat pegs, calendars and picture hooks haphazard the walls.

Exterior, the sheds and fences lean. An old boneshaker of a bicycle is propped up against the House. A country mailbox, lettered EVERETT LEWIS, could stand on a post by the Road. In the distance stands the Poor Farm, a prison for the poor, written about more fully in my play *The Poor Farm*, the second in the trilogy. The Poor Farm is not seen but affects the Maud Lewis House. The presentation of Maud's images is once again within the province of the Director. Projections might be shown in blackouts. Colour posters of Maud's pictures from my books (Kinko's does a good job) might be hung in the theatre lobby. The pictures completed in the course of the play might be slightly oversize for better viewing by the audience. It's amazing they well they show up from a distance. In addition to the warming oven, Maud often placed, on a sunny day, her paintings on the storm door facing the Road. This may be viewed, together with her sign, *Paintings for Sale*, in the documentary film *The Illuminated Life of Maud Lewis*, of which I wrote the script.

The second play in this trilogy, *The Poor Farm* (The Charles Press, Halifax, Nova Scotia, 1996) might be of interest. It certainly cost me enough. All these houses, buildings, institutions, codes, laws and characters may be found at greater length in my novel *Asylum Road*.

### Lighting
The lighting in both community and professional productions has been inventive and surprising. Parts of this play are recollected in the memory of our characters: These recollections might be suggested by sombre Black and White. The battle scenes and all the struggles spinning from Maud's pictures might be more brightly lit: all this within the province of the lighting designer and the director.

# Act One

**Greetings:** *A Woman for Keep*
The Judge scuffs through an abandoned House.

**Act 1 Scene 1** *The Three Black Cats*
Maud hides her work in the warming oven of the range.

**Act 1 Scene 2** *The Judge Recalls the Trade*
The last sale of the year.

**Act 1 Scene 3** *Bert Saws Bill Out of the Wall*
A visit both commercial and kindly.

**Act 1 Scene 4** *The End of the Spanish Dancers*
Ev comes home to find Bill gone.

**Act 1 Scene 5** *Big Junior Offers a Winter's Wood*
The spectre of the Poor Farm hangs over the house.

**Act 1 Scene 6** *Graves Open, Ghosts Escape Like Whispers and Fearful Secrets Visit*
A visit sparks an argument lodged in the past.

**Act 1 Scene 7** *The Judge of the Wealth of the World*
The Three Black Cats goes to a little girl.

# Act Two

**Act 2 Scene 1**  *The Sermon to the Ash*
Maud thanks Junior for the winter's wood.

**Act 2 Scene 2**  *Little Juny in the Evening*
Juny sees the inside. Ev visits a treasure.

**Act 2 Scene 3**  *The Painting Lesson*
Maud passes along a mother's gift.

**Act 2 Scene 4**  *Ev and Bert Tangle*
Bert returns with the bonus on Bill.

**Act 2 Scene 5**  *The Remedy*
Maud's feet go up in the oven.

**Act 2 Scene 6**  *The Last One That She Did*
Juny's bluebirds go south.

**Act 2 Scene 7**  *The Finest Roses in the County*
The Three Black Cats returns.

**Act 2 Scene 8**  *Big Junior's Book of Acts*
A chowder and a partridge get to the step.

**Act 2 Scene 9**  *Maud Asks a Favour*
Ev steals away. Maud fills the empty chair in the nativity.

Maud Lewis World Without Shadows

# GREETINGS

*It is evening and the church bells ring. The house is dark and desolate. It looks abandoned. Prevailing light: Black and White.*

*A few leaves fall to the ground to the sound of a Gibson guitar. A light fades in: The Judge roots all around the rotting house. What is he looking for?*

*He finds a wooden square, and examines it with satisfaction. What is it?*

**THE JUDGE**
There it is!

*Paintings for Sale revealed.*

I knew if I kept looking.

*Great satisfaction. He wonders if he has been seen.*

It was Everett put the ad in the paper. Everett. Ev. Wanted: A woman for her keep. Her room and board. Room and board in a one room house.

*A long, thin finger cocked to the House. In light, the butterflies and bees shine on the old storm door. In light, the House glitters like Christmas. Windows and decorations gleam.*

She walked from town and long that road. The dead a night. That's how she came to leave Aunt Ida's. Aunt Ida, well, she couldn't stand men.

*He thinks.*

That's understandable. Maud stepped up and knocked rate on that door, the dog he never said a single word. Ev looked out the window in the door, and couldn't see her. She was just a little thing. A cripple.

*He mimes her disability.*

She'd hide her hands. But. If you teased her then those hands would spring up to her mouth. Afraid to speak. Afraid to laugh. I'd keep teasing, first thing you know then she'd be smiling.

*He smiles. His caricature relaxes. He hangs the Sign up on the House. He returns to the audience. He twists a silver ring.*

Ev would get himself upset. Jealous. If you spent your time with Maud. Everett. A bent nail. Jealous, just about anything. Take the batteries out of the radio. Wrap them up in old wax paper. He rationed music.

Paintings for Sale.

*That stabbing finger at the Sign.*

It hung right there, to face the Road. Ev sat Maud out by the Road to fetch the trade. The cars would slow rate down: What am I looking at?

*He impersonates astonishment.*

Half an hour, she'd be covered in the dust. Ev played the pity game. Maud preferred her little corner. You in your small corner. I in mine.

*He smiles.*

The day she come back in. Hell to pay.

*A recollection.*

But she never went back out. That sunny corner come to be her world.

*The eyebrows lift. He stops by the axe in the block, and attempts to lift it. It sticks. He gives up on the axe.*

He kept the dogs down there. A wire cage. Ev would tell you, fact, the dogs loved him, not Maud. The strangest thing. Ev killed his little rabbit dog two days before the murder. Good little rabbit dog. Soft mouth. Ev said "You kin do anything to her and she will love you." Out of Bill and Beaut as I recall. Bill was a gift from Doctor Dickie. Ev spoke well of every dog he had.

*He surveys the scene.*

Once. Here. Rate here.

*He points to ground.*

I told a ghost, you can't come back. You can't never come back home! What can you tell a ghost.

*They're unreliable.*

Once it starts, you can't stop it.

> *The Judge sticks his tongue out of his mouth and shakes his head.*
> *Death is beyond his jurisdiction.*

> *Bert Potter from the Road. Bert and the Judge stand apart but pay attention to their stories. The ghosts agree with some, but not all.*

**BERT**
Ev. Was kilt. Struck dead and never got up.

> *The origin of violence.*

Maud made the money and Ev made trouble.

> *The Judge to the sheds at the back of the House.*

Maud Lewis. Famous. For decades, she would never cross the Road. Could not go over to the neighbours for a quiet cup of tea. And there he kept her.

> *The House.*

Couldn't go across it for a quiet cup of tea.

> *The Road.*

Maud Lewis. Spent the whole of every day, painting little pictures. As fast as she could get them done, then they were gone. Dear little thing, she was some little! Back, twisted. Hunchback was the word.

> *The light of a kerosene lamp appears in the window of Maud's corner. Colour seeps into the Black and White. Maud appears in the window.*

But her eyes, bright! And what a smile.

> *A grimace disappoints. Maud to the step and into the sun. An artist's brush. She touches up the Sign. An errant stroke is tidied with a tip of her apron. The sound of a motor on the old dirt road. A horn toots. Maud turns to wave. And then she smiles. And then, the dust, she coughs. The Judge returns with an apple crate. He sets it beneath the sign.*

**THE JUDGE**

Children, hid in the ditch, right-along here. To spy on the crooked old witch. Her little house, the jail, a Hansel and Gretel. Res ipsa lockit her up, the prison was next door, the Poor Farm, where I, as magistrate, you understand, had the solemn duty to.

*He chooses his words.*

Place the Poor. You understand.

*He points and nods.*

My obligation. And. My solemn jurisdiction. Ever-ett Lewis. Ev. Night Watchman at the Poor Farm. The proper name, as I expect you know, was the Alms House. But nobody could, e-nun-ciate "Alms House." The word got stuck. So we just called it by The Poor Farm.

The harmless poor and all the unwed mothers a the county. Caught em out. Looked after them. The question of their county settlement. Kept me busy. The violent was locked up in the basement.

*The Judge twists a remarkable ring on his pointing finger.*

Night Watchman to the Poor Farm poor. Ev. A dollar for every night he walked the wards and stairs. Trouble there. But. Who else would do that for a dollar?

*He thinks about that. Maud sweeps the step with a corn broom.*

Maud Dowley, Lewis was her married name. Spent the first day cleaning up the cans Ev just used to toss'em out the window. That might explain the anthill by the step.

*Maud sweeps the ants from her shoes. The Judge gestures to the magnificent vista.*

A look out here. The hill by the range, maples and ash. White birch and linden. Come autumn, all in colour, red and gold. Autumn leaves. And below, the Field, the earth so deep that you could drive a spade down anywheres and never hit a stone. Hay from the marsh. The best, and endless.

Along the shore, the wharf and beach. The packet Princess. There the Bay, the richest fishery in all the world. Scallops and lobsters. Haddock and cod. The herring and the mackerel in shoals. Great shoals! The weir. Fished well.

I never had to work. I went to school I had it nailed. I took the law.

The Wharf there, where they landed fish on shares, five thousand pounds a trip. Just below the Poor Farm. Odd, ain't it. Hard by the Church a God. Odd. Ain't it.

*Maud touches up the heart on the door. A red drop running down.*

**BERT**
The House was oh ten feet by twelve. Oh more or less. Mostly less. Not a straight line anywheres. A ladder on the kitchen wall to get up to the loft. And later, when she come, Ev built a stairs. You'd get the shakes, just watching her, get up and down those stairs. Ev liked the ladder better. He'd get excited, forget the stairs. Go up the wall a spider on the ladder to the loft.

*Points up and down.*

He was a strange man.

*Maud cleans her hands on her apron and enters the House. She sits, interior and looks out the window.*

No running water, no telephone, no e-lec-tri-cal. The range, a firebox for wood, that's all they had. A warming oven on the top. Biscuits in the oven of the range, when Ev allowed the baking powder. We tried, I'm talking Keith and I, to put them in a bathroom on the south. A pump there for a sink, a toilet at the back, but Ev – he would not have it. He knew exactly what he wanted.

The second day that she was here, Maud was bit by a widow spider. Ev got a can of Raid. And sprayed. All up and down her legs and come that close to killing her rate there. Day Number two! To the end, he would not have a screen door on the House. She suffered from the black flies while she tried to work.

She used to walk the back path to the Poor Farm. Take a bath on Tuesdays for the Harmless Poor. The Certified, she stayed at home. You wouldn't want to take a bath with the Insane. The Harmless was on Tuesday. And when she got a bath, the matron, Olive, used to do her hair. I spoke to Olive on the day Maud died. And Olive said: I hope to say that we were friends.

**THE JUDGE**
Outside a path a clam shells, white in the sun. The shells would crunch beneath your boots. Pretty that path, with a border of sweet peas. You got to give to Ev his due. The man could grow a pea.

*He thinks.*

Maud had a Sullivan cousin could carve a endless chain from a one-piece block of wood. Clear through and solid, perfect grain. Human beans are not like that.

*A sigh.*

We're all mistaken.

*He shrugs. The Judge makes off with the Sign and the crate. Bert watches his departure. Maud straightens her apron. She takes the Three Black Cats from the tray. She struggles to place it up to the warming oven. She peeks, carefully, beyond the curtains of her window.*

**BERT**
You look back now you wonder why we didn't see it coming. Those years.

*An appeal.*

But at the time. Well, they were man and wife. The theft of years. Murder ain't the half of it. What could you do?

*Two guitars. A country tune. Bert looks to the house but fails to approach. A smile to the audience.*

How are you fixed for forgiveness?

*Bert looks in her purse, finds a note, reads it, clucks her tongue and off to the Road to wander. Darkness descends, leaving the only light to the little corner. Maud works away.*

*And then two hands appear to close the curtains.*

*ACT ONE SCENE ONE*

# THREE BLACK CATS

*Ev from the woods.Sunshine and colour. Two rabbits swing by a
cord strung through their ankles. Maud turns off the radio.*

**MAUD**
Ev?

> *He ignores her.*

Please.

> *He ignores her.*

Those rabbits, are dripping.

> *Ev scuffs the blood into the floor.*

**EV**
I just caught em.

> *Can't she see the obvious? Maud cleans the blood up with a rag.
> Newspaper from the woodbox.*

**MAUD**
Could you gut them on the step?

**EV**
Sure. Sure, I could. If I wanted, then I would.

> *He looks at her strangely.*

A thousand rabbits cleaned rate here.

> *He looks to see if she understands.*

It's cold out there. You see, their coats are changing.

I dragged this house to here. Me, Lonny and, and Bump. And four
span a oxen. That makes, what? Was Bump, wasn't it. Bumper. God
Rest His Ragged Soul. He should be soon be getting out.

> *She returns the rag to a bucket.*

Mine before you ever set foot here.

*Ev hangs the rabbits from a hook above the stove. Maud turns to save the Three Black Cats from blood. He watches carefully. The Black Cabinet swings open. He takes a lock from a shelf and closes the door and locks it. He likes the click of the snap of the lock.*

**MAUD**
This one's still wet.

*Maud displays The Three Black Cats.*

**EV**
Nobody will ever buy that! You got to paint a pixture with a ox. A ox in it.
A ox. A span. That's what they likes! I wonder you don't listen.

*The Cats protective in her hands.*

**MAUD**
This one is spoken for. Little black cats.

**EV**
Why do I bother to scavenge those boards. You never listen.

**MAUD**
This one is sold.

**EV**
You're off your rocker.

**MAUD**
The Judge himself. He wants it and he's coming by. He spoke for it.

**EV**
You're lying. Or you're off your rocker.

*She shows him the painting.*

I hope you're lying.

*She shakes her head "no."*

Why would anyone want cats! An ox! That's what they want. Well? Well?

*She waits him out.*
**MAUD**
I hear you Ev.

*He advances. She retreats.*

**EV**

Black cats! Bad luck! Cats belong with the rats in a barn.

**MAUD**

I had a cat Miss B lived in my room.

**EV**

Well there you go! Look at yah! Well, look at yah! Just look. You know what cats do to a child?

> *She lowers the painting. Defeated. She places it in her chair in the sunny corner. And then courage.*

**MAUD**

The Judge has spoken for it, for his littlest girl. She lost her kitten to the Road.

**EV**

The Judge! Why would the Judge want a picture a cats.

**MAUD**

For his littlest girl. For her. He cares about her.

> *She nods. He gapes.*

He spoke for it. I'll clean it up.

> *Ev doesn't want it cleaned up. He finds a jacknife in his overalls. He shakes his head.*

**EV**

They're just laughing, don't you know. Don't you know. They laugh at us. They do! They do. Don't you hear the things they say?

> *He sticks the knife in the table. He seizes the Cats.*

I'll scrape it. I'll scrape it off, you start on over. This picture. Ain't going to sell. A real good board that I got off the dump.

> *He displays the board.*

**MAUD**

I'll put in a ox!

> *He tries to jam it into the fire box.*

**EV**

Too big!

*The Cats to the woodbox.*

Can't you do nothing? Feeding the birds! On account a you, the drainpipe is plugged with birdshit.

*He waves to the heavens.*

The Flood will come and I'll be happy.

**MAUD**
Well, the Flood would clear the drainpipe.

*Is she crazy? Is this treason? He gapes. He scuttles up the ladder to the loft. She seizes the Cats from the woodbox. She hides it in the oven of the range. He twists and bends. Maud speaks to his legs.*

**MAUD**
How about? A cup of tea?

*Ev descends with Oxen in a Summer Bower.*
**EV**
There! See! That's the ticket!

*Raps on the board.*

Struck gold on that one! That's what they want! They'll buy every single, solitary one. All you got to do is churn them out.

*The Oxen on the table.*

Just finish this. It needs a leg. Just get a leg on that one somewhere. Someone sees that on the door, they'll stop and buy it. What was I doing?

*He seizes the knife. And the rabbits from the hanging hook. She fetches the newspapers.*
**MAUD**
Ev, please.

**EV**
Oh my good-gone-along Moses.

*The knife at the Oxen.*

That's the ticket. Don't you forget it.

*He thinks. He takes the newspapers against the blood.*

Clean the rabbits. Scrape the cats.

*He points, with the blade, to the woodbox. The jack-knife to a satisfying click. The rabbits swing. He strides behind the House. The dog barks.*

I'm coming!

*Maud waits. And then she quietly, carefully takes the Cats out of the oven. She cleans, with her apron, a drop or two of blood. She returns it to the oven and quietly, carefully closes the door. A peek out the window.*

*To dark.*

## ACT ONE SCENE TWO

# THE JUDGE RECALLS THE TOURIST TRADE

*Ev fetches boughs to bank the House. He wears a red wool cap with flaps and strings. He tamps the boughs down with his feet. The Judge returns to watch Ev dance. A dog barks. The Oxen is displayed on the storm door. The Judge speaks to the audience.*

**THE JUDGE**
He knew each and every trick. Bank the House with boughs against the winter. Low tide and herring there left hanging in the weir. What orchard wild, but bearing. He had his woodpile stacked a year ahead. Ev believed, that he was the boss of the business. Constant badgering. Maud had to wait for Ev to go somewheres.

*The Judge roots around. Big Junior enters with a cross-cut saw. He sits on a stump with the saw and a file.*

**THE JUDGE**
The Sign alone would bring them in.

**BIG JUNIOR**
You best watch the Judge, you best.

*A motor. Junior turns.*

**THE JUDGE**
They came looking for a little old lady. But when they pulled up by the Road they had, Everett, to deal with.

*He recollects a commonplace visit. He calls the lines without turning about.*

**THE JUDGE IN RECOLLECTION OF A TOURIST**

Hello there!

**EV**
Hello yourself.

**THE JUDGE**
The weather this cold <u>all</u> the time?

**EV**
Some times.

**THE JUDGE**
This here your house?

**EV**
Who says it ain't?

>           *Junior laughs.*

**THE JUDGE**
It's awful small.

**EV**
It's bigger than it looks. That's her in there.

**THE JUDGE**
I'll take this one. How much?

>           *Ev jumps up with his hand out.*

**EV**
She don't touch cash. It's her religion.

>           *Ev spins. Two dollar bills appear in his hand. He holds them up
>           in triumph. The Judge whispers.*

**THE JUDGE**
Where do you sleep?

**EV**
I learned to do without it.

>           *The Judge declaims.*

**THE JUDGE**

There's only three legs on this left-hand ox.

**EV**
The last one is behind, its behind.

>           *Ev hauls on the chain to his wallet. He pulls it up from his
>           overalls like a man hauling up a bucket from a well. He gives
>           each bill a snap, deposits all, zips up the zipper and lowers all.*

**THE JUDGE**
It's safe enough in there.

**EV**
I guess it is.

> *Ev to the House. The Judge turns from the audience. He collects the Oxen and departs. Maud enters carrying a pitcher.*

**BIG JUNIOR**
And that was Everett Lewis. Whose father lost their farm out in Bear River. Poorest type, like myself! And died beneath another name. And Ev a child, a prisoner in the Poor Farm with his mother Mary. You could say he never left. So you can't be too hard. On anyone. You'd be making a mistake.

> *A mystery strikes.*

Why we come back here.

> *He shakes his head. Ev peers at the departing tourists. Maud tries an encouraging smile.*

**MAUD**
They bought a board.

**EV**
We got to sell way more than one.

> *Buttoning his pockets*

Jumping old frog-legged Jacob, Maud. You're the one that went to school.

> *Muttering*

Three legs on a ox! You could a lost it all.

> *Maud laughs. Hands to her mouth. Ev to the well. Maud follows with the pitcher. He tosses a bucket on a rope down the well.*

**EV**
Sorry, Fred! Almost hit yah.

> *He turns to Maud.*

Talking to the trout.

**MAUD**
I know.

**EV**
In the well.

**MAUD**
I know.

**EV**
Get fat! With luck, you might just see the spring.

> *Turns to Maud.*

I'm talking to the trout.

**MAUD**
I know.

> *Ev empties water into the pitcher. He takes a cracker out of a pocket, eats half and crumbles the rest to Fred. Maud to the door with the pitcher. She stops to see if he is off to Andy Perry's store, or, perhaps, Lloyd Grant's.*

**MAUD**
We're low on milk.

> *He slips a basket from a limb over the handlebars.*

**EV**
Yeah, yeah.

**MAUD**
Don't go anywheres near the Farm.

**EV**
Yeah, yeah.

> *He ties the red flaps under his chin.*

**MAUD**
There he goes wobble off to town.

> *She calls out.*

Watch out for the ditch!

*She enters the House, sets the pitcher down and returns with*
*a sable brush. She straightens the sign, Paintings for Sale. She*
*smiles to the bluebird mama and brightens with a sable from her*
*apron a breast of pale yellow and ochre. To the House to sit in*
*the window. The radio.*
*And to her work.*

**MAUD**

A board and paints, and I'm alright. I'm not much for going places
anyways. And I look out to see who comes.

*All to gray. She looks out the window and back to her work. Big*
*Junior stands. The saw upon his shoulder.*

**BIG JUNIOR**

I never knew whether he loved her or not. I couldn't make it out.
Maybe he loved her when she came. And then he found out she
could make that money.

*He thinks.*

For now we see through a glass darkly. That's from the Bible. The
sufferings abound. You don't need to go to Macedonia.

*Junior exits.*

## ACT ONE SCENE THREE

# BERT SAWS BILL OUT OF THE WALL

*The sound of a motor. It stops. Bert walks the path of shells.*
*Maud withdraws. Bert knocks on the door. No reply.*
*Bert taps on a window pane. She opens the door.*

**BERT**
Maud dear. Are you at home?

**MAUD**
That you, Bert?

**BERT**
Just me.

> *Maud descends from the loft. Bert enters and closes the door.*

**MAUD**
I guess you must a got a new truck.

> *Bert knows Maud has been hiding. She smiles.*

**BERT**
Maud dear you don't have to hide from me. Was not about to stop, but I saw Everett on the Road.

> *She laughs and waves to the road.*

**MAUD**
How was he doing?

**BERT**
Well, he was vertical.

> *A smile. Bert holds a little tin of aspirin.*

Here, dear.

**MAUD**
Oh, thank you! For your kindness. It's been bad.

> *She fears her bones are worse.*

I can pay you when the Old Age comes.

> *Bert waives the payment. Maud slips the aspirin into her apron pocket. She kneads her misshapen hands.*

I wish he would give up the wheel. Down he goes! Off goes the crows and over the corn.

> *Maud's hands describe the flight of the crows. And then she hides her hands within an apron fold.*

I wish he never sold the Model T.

**BERT**
Maybe that was for the best.

> *Maud shifts the kettle for a pot of tea. Bert begins a tour about the House.*

Maud you got bluebirds on your windowsill. Just like the song. Can't sell your windowsill my dear. Here's something new.

> *Bert finds The Three Black Cats atop the warming oven.*

**MAUD**
The Judge wanted kittens for a birthday.

**BERT**
My glasses.

> *Bert searches for her glasses. The purse. No specs. She noses the board. Maud on tip-toe: the paint from Bert's nose with her apron.*

**MAUD**
It's not quite dry.

**BERT**
My nose?

> *They laugh.*

**MAUD**
The board. It's not quite done. And what it wants. Is blossoms.

**BERT**
Blossoms.

**MAUD**

Like heaven. I allus thought that heaven would be blossoms.

**BERT**

I'm sure it will be. Just for you. The Judge wants this one, does he?

    *Maud nods.*

First come, first served.

    *Bert picks up the Cats. She steps into sunlight for a better look.*
    *Maud is caught between two friends.*

And here I am.

**MAUD**

Oh! I can't Bert. That one's for the Judge's little girl. She lost her
kitten, poor thing, poor thing.

    *Bert returns the board to the storm door. She cleans her fingers*
    *with a tissue.*

**BERT**

Listen. We have a grandchild on the way.

**MAUD**

Oh Bert! Good news!

**BERT**

So. How about, a baby in a cradle. A cradle and a Christmas tree.

**MAUD**

A basket. With the sweet grass woven in.

    *A conspiracy of inspiration.*

**BERT**

Candles on the lowering boughs!

**MAUD**

For that, I'd want a real good board.

    *Bert thinks.*

**BERT**

Now, what kind a board?

**MAUD**

I've been painting on that cardboard.

    *She whispers.*

They're not keeping Everett on. We're losing a dollar every day that we get up.

**BERT**
I hear they're going to shut it down.

*Maud turns away. Bert turns her around.*

We heard. Well then. Night Watchman at the Poor Farm. There's worse to lose than that.

**MAUD**
A dollar a day.

**BERT**
I can get you wallboard. Sawed up square.

*This is hopeful news.*

**MAUD**
The back a wallboard takes the paint.

**BERT**
It doesn't warp or twist. Tell you what, we'll get you all the wallboard you can use.

*She nods in finality.*

And sawed up square. Keith will see-to-it. A dollar a day is nothing to what you can make right here.

*Bert taps the walls. A squawking.*

**MAUD**
That's just the chickens. On the back.

**BERT**
You'd think the man could build a chicken coop. Well, I got to go.

*Yet Bert stops. The decorated walls inspire a thought. She taps the wall with a finger.*

**MAUD**
That was Bill. Old Bill. Nobody come along that road without he give a bark. Bill. Ev's old favourite.

**BERT**
You got a paring knife?

*Slow business and deadly intent.*

**MAUD**
Don't know how sharp.

*A knife. Bert stabs the wall. A squawk from the flock. Bert procedes to saw Bill out of the wall. Maud is amazed.*

**MAUD**
Bert! My girl!

**BERT**
What in the name!

**MAUD**
I think you hit a hen was on the nest.

*Unfazed, Bert thumps the handle. One word to match each thump.*

**BERT**
Lathe. Bark. And plaster dust.

*Sneezes. Bert rubs her nose. Maud assesses the damage.*

**MAUD**
Oh Bert. Ev hates a draft.

*Bert questions this.*

A Indian said he'd die of a chill. And turn black from the toes on up.

**BERT**
I'd risk that.

*She resumes the cut and thumping.*

You got the last house in the County.

*An effort.*

Packed with birchbark. What's this?

**MAUD**

Eelgrass.

**BERT**

I got a frame, will fit this dog.

**MAUD**

I just painted Bill to cheer Ev up. One day he.

**BERT**

He'll never know.

**MAUD**

Who?

**BERT**

And what's more.

**MAUD**

Bill?

> *Bert waves to the Road.*

**BERT**

Him. I'm talking about that man.

> *Bert lifts the wallpaper. She turns. But Maud is anxious.*

I'll frame it and sell it as a picture.

**MAUD**

That?

**BERT**

And sell it at the store.

> *Bert seizes a Star Weekly from the woodbox. She rips a leaf –
> an illustration of two Spanish dancers. Bert takes a brush and
> paints the back and slaps it on the hole.*

**BERT**

And don't you tell that man a yours. About this ten.

> *Bert selects ten dollars from her purse. Maud is astonished. She
> hides it under the bag in the sugar tin.*

What a man don't know. Don't matter. Without you, Maud, nobody in
the county would ever even. Darken that door. How you been feeling
anyways?

**MAUD**
Oh, up and down. The nights are getting pretty sharp.

*A hug from Bert. Bert glances at the clock.*

**BERT**
Is that the time?

**MAUD**
No, that's last week.

**BERT**
What?

**MAUD**
It stopped. We got to get some kerosene to clean the works.

**BERT**
Well, just you remember. We're all living on the same one road. That ten dollars is for you. And waiting when you need it.

*She gives the tin to Maud. She rolls up Bill.*

There's plenty more where that ten come from. And you know where? From you.

*She pats Maud's hands about the sugar tin.*
It's you.

**MAUD**
But Bert.

**BERT**
I'll get those boards made up. And we're in business.

*Maud bites her lip.*

No charge.

*Bert points to the Sign.*

Don't ever let His Honour git that sign. That man can't keep his hands off anything.

*Bert straightens her dress and flounces out. She waves good-bye with Bill. Maud salutes the door and watches Bert drive off. A wave to the departing truck. She places the tin back on the shelf.*

*And then she walks to inspect the Spanish Dancers. She taps the edges into the paper and paint. She stops in front of the sugar tin and stares.*

**MAUD**
Oh my. How's he going to take to this.

## ACT ONE SCENE FOUR

# THE END OF THE SPANISH DANCERS

*Maud lights the lamp in her corner. She settles down to work. A glance or two escapes to the Spanish Dancers. Ev to the yard, bicycle and basket. She hears a scrape on the step.*

**MAUD**
Well. Here he is.

*She rises to greet at the door.*

Everett.

**EV**
Hold on a minute.

*The hat flaps dangle. Ev places a pint of milk on the table.*

There it is, milk! And just like gold. Ten trucks passed me on the road! Bert Potter ducked way down and sped on by. Makes you wonder what kind of people people are.

*A hand on the table to steady his legs.*

The wind was agin me. But I held on.

*She nearly touches him.*

**MAUD**
Wait till you see.

*Ev attends to his clothes and boots. He sits. He groans. He spies the Spanish Dancers. He leaps.*

**EV**
What the lord lifting?

*To Maud for an explanation.*

**MAUD**
Well. It wasn't the Lord.

*Ev, sockfoot and boot, steps to the wall. He looks at it, pokes it and spins for an answer.*

**EV**

Come home to a hole in the nor-east wall.

**MAUD**

It's not like, what it looks.

**EV**

Well it looks like what it looks like.

**MAUD**

No, no! It's in the tin.

> *Maud struggles to reach the tin. Her hands are like a vine grown wrong. She holds the tin to her chest. Her twisted fingers can't open the tin. They scratch against the lid.*

**EV**

You want some sugar?

**MAUD**

You'll never believe what happened.

**EV**

You got that right.

> *Maud holds out the sugar tin. Ev takes the tin and pops the lid. He lifts the bag. The fabulous cash.*

**EV**

I'm going to go down! And buy ever bag of sugar they got left.

> *He thinks, then whispers.*

Do they know?

**MAUD**

No no! It's ours! Bert Potter come along.

> *Maud points to the Spanish Dancers.*

**EV**

A woman should never hide money from her husband. I took you. You got your keep. You got to keep up your end a the bargain. A woman got to listen to the man it's in the Bible. Like when Bill's Beaut strayed to the road I whistled up and Beauty come back.

*Distress. He breathes heavily.*

Beauty was a good, good dog. Bite anybody.

> *Maud laughs.*

**MAUD**
Well, I'm not <u>biting</u> anyone.

> *He holds the ten dollars to the heavens. He waves it to the syllables.*

**EV**
Where. Did. This TEN DOLLARS come from.

**MAUD**
Ev. Ev. This ten dollars. Is from Bert Potter.

> *She points down the road.*

**EV**
Bert Potter?

> *Maud nods.*

Keith Potter's Bert Potter?

**MAUD**
Yes.

**EV**
Keith Potter's Bert Potter runs the store.

**MAUD**
Yes.

**EV**
Keith Potter's Bert Potter passed me on the highway?

**MAUD**
Yup.

**EV**
What the dickens did <u>she</u> want?

**MAUD**
Bill.

**EV**
Bill! Bill is dead!

> *Maud shakes her head but cannot speak.*

You dug up Bill?

> *The kind of crazy thing that women do. Yet here is proof: Ten Dollars.*
> *He looks to the window. Maud gathers herself for the gathering storm.*

**MAUD**
No, no. Ev. Sit-Sit. Sit before you blow a gasket.

> *They settle in the lamplight. Ev grasps the tin with one hand, the cash with the other.*

Bert just wanted to buy the Cats. The Judge already spoke for it. So I couldn't sell the Cats to Bert. So Bert, sawed Bill. Out of the wall.

**EV**
I remember Bill!

> *He jumps up again. To the wall.*

He's gone!

**MAUD**
Bert gave me the ten for the picture a Bill.

> *Determination.*

I will do her up another. She's good for it.

> *Ev gives this serious consideration. But fear wins.*

**EV**
I'd rather starve.

**MAUD**
We're close.

**EV**
You let that that woman come ripsaw up my house? Howard. Whole. Dead Elijah! Come home some day and the front door will be gone. We'll perish of the dry heaves where we stand. Stone! Cold! Drifting Moses in the Rushes Desperate.

**MAUD**
Hold on now.

**EV**
Come home, northwind and look right out! We'll starve, freeze, heave
and die. We'll die rate here in our underwear! Rate where we spit and
sleep! I might as well just curl up now and close my eyes. Give me
two pennies all I want! We might as well just curl-up-twist-up-and
fall together now!

> *He throws himself on the settee in the corner. Maud waits.*

**MAUD**
I can always paint another dog.

> *Ev halts. He peers at Maud. Can this tale of wealth be true? He
> rattles, for his comfort, the cash within his hand. He sets the
> sugar tin aside.*
> *He breathes on the ten dollar bill.*

**EV**
It's real. We had a close one. A close-on-one.

> *Hesitating.*

Theft and death. Death and theft. They allus go together.

> *Ev blinks at Maud in emphasis. She answers with patient
> quietness and kindness.*

**MAUD**
In the first place, Bert never killed Bill. She done her best but he died
on the hearth. In the second place, she did not steal his picture. She
paid ten dollars for the picture. There it is.

**EV**
They steal from you, they got to lie. That's true.

**MAUD**
She never said a word against us. She heard about our troubles.

**EV**
I'm not talking bout Bert Potter. I'm talking about Everyone.

> *An involuntary shudder. A mutter.*

**MAUD**
Honest dollars.

**EV**
Supposing I was just to just go down there walk right into Keith's new house and saw a hole in his south wall and give him ten new dollars!

> *Patient and kind.*

**MAUD**
I would expect, he'd be surprised.

> *Ev stands. He strips the Dancers off the wall. It sticks in his hand.*
> *He burns the Dancers in the stove. Light from the firebox.*

**MAUD**
You got to calm on down. Ten dollars for a picture. That's more than fair.

> *Ev cleans his hands with a rag off the stove.*

**EV**
Hell will freeze. Before I could trust that. Woman.

> *He deposits the ten in his wallet.*

Crisp as grass. Keith must get his money from the Bank.

> *Maud watches the rise and fall of the money. Ev points at the hole in the wallpaper.*

Houdini. Himself. Could not fix that!

> *Maud shifts The Three Black Cats. She hangs it over the hole on a hat peg.*

**MAUD**
Everett. The most we get most times is two.

> *She nods at the cats.*

Ten dollars. Now, we can get a little money for the winter.

**EV**
You must think. That I'm, a. Fo-o-ol.

*To the Cats. An accusatory finger to the Cats, and then to Maud.*

When then is she coming back?

**MAUD**
She didn't say.

*Maud ladles water to the kettle.*

**EV**
We had a close one! But I can handle the likes of her.

*To matrimony.*

Bring her in, is she grateful? Keep the secrets, where does it get yah?

*Ev unties the hat flaps. To plead fatigue, he sighs. He takes a tea bag out of the tin, and checks the tin for cash. He cuts the bag and sprinkles leaves into the pot.*

Live tea. That Potter woman. Is like a lawyer. If they allowed a woman at the law, she'd be one.

*Maud pours a drop of milk into the mug and the cup.*

Whoa there!

*Startled, Maud drops the pint. Shock. Ev stares at the stream. Maud hides her hands. Ev paddles and spoons the milk into the bottle.*

**MAUD**
Oh!

*She tries to assist.*

**EV**
Sit down. You've done enough for one day. If anybody, ever, told me I'd be living with a cripple. I would have said - they should be <u>taken in</u>.

*He looks at Maud. She tries to stand straight.*

Hah!

*She tries again to straighten her back.*

Not workin. Who'd look after you but me?

Jumping pumpkins! Forgot the rabbits!

> *Maud takes her tea to her corner. Ev to the yard in haste to hunt about the woodpile. Disaster. She looks out the window as he shouts. Ev through the door.*

Two good rabbits. Stolen by stoats!

> *A revelation from behind his back.*

And. One dead red hen!

> *He throws the pile of feathers into the woodbox. He returns disconsolate to the chair by the table. Maud sets down her tea. She approaches the table. She waits. Ev explodes.*

**EV**
How can you eat it if you don't know what killed it!

> *She adds a drop or two of tea to Everett's cup.*

**MAUD**
We're doing all right.

> *Nil from Ev.*

We're doing better. I much prefer the water from the running brook. Don't you. It makes a better cup of tea. Don't you think. Especially live tea.

> *Defeated, he sits by the table. He speaks in a low, continuous rumble. She quietly shifts his cup of tea forward.*

**EV**
I'm surrounded. There's more women in the world than men. A man can't get ahead.

**MAUD**
Not every day that we make ten dollars.

> *Ev nods his head. The thought cheers him up.*

**EV**
When Bert comes back, you got to have one ready.

**MAUD**
I will.

> *He begins to cheer up.*

We never made as much as ten before. I can hardly believe it.

> *Ev agrees.*

**EV**
The way you paint. What one does she want?

**MAUD**
The Christmas Child.

> *Of which Ev knows little.*

We just made it up. A Christmas Baby in a cradle. She's going to bring me the board.

**EV**
What's she want for that?

**MAUD**
Nothing.

> *Ev snorts. She nods.*

**EV**
You never painted that one before.

**MAUD**
I think that I can do it.

> *On to something more important.*

**EV**
I wasn't planning on killing that hen. Until they ate up all those husks.

**MAUD**
You can buy a dozen chicks now from the Doucettes.

> *He looks in the direction of The Dancers.*

**EV**
Ten Dollar Bill. That's how I'll always think of him.

> *A sigh. A glance to the wall.*

Bill and Beauty. Now there was a pair. Those two around nobody wants to cut holes in the house.

*A thought strikes.*

What did the Judge want?

**MAUD**
The Cats. The picture of the tabby and her kittens. He wants it for his little girl. It's for her birthday.

**EV**
You never told me that!

*She chooses peace.*

**MAUD**
Escape my mind.

**EV**
See there you go. I told you it was gone. Well then. Take stock.
There's the Cats.
Bill. Bert.

*Counts on his fingers.*

One. Two.

*He gives up.*
*He stops at three fingers.*
**MAUD**
Three.

**EV**
No no. I know. But how much is that?

*It's hopeless.*

We'll charge the Judge ten dollars. Same as her.

*Weary. That's all a man can do! A summary. A sigh. To a wooden barrel.*

There's nothing left but herring.

*Maud hopes to ask a favour.*

**MAUD**
Could you take the head off mine?

*He nods. Ev up to his elbows, herring in the pickle of a barrel.*

*Their slippery selves elude. He compares two herring.*

**EV**
What's ten to the Living Judge? O let him twist his silver ring, I'm charging ten!

> *Maud sits in her corner, sipping her tea, happy to share in the recovery.*
> *He tosses the heads to the firebox. He shifts the iron dampers.*

**MAUD**
I'm sorry on the milk.

**EV**
A shock like that can stop yah in your tracks. Like when you drop a clock, can't even talk about it. Ten bucks for a cut-out off the walls. Wasn't even a real good board.

> *Crafty.*

How many can you do a day?

> *He peels a potato and drops it into the pot on the range.*

I got a piece a cardboard.

> *She is very tired.*

How are yah feeling?

> *She warms her hands on the teacup.*

**MAUD**
I could try.

> *Hopeful of rest.*

Ev?

**EV**
What?

**MAUD**
Your boots.

**EV**
Oh.

> *He removes a boot and slips into his slippers. The boots behind the stove.*

**MAUD**

The Judge is coming back tomorrow.

> *Light to her hands as she rubs her fingers. Ev drops a piece of*
> *cardboard from the woodbox to her tray.*

**EV**

This is a real good piece of cardboard. A little bent. I got it off a
dressbox off a Wright's.

> *Maud looks at the cardboard. On one side an illustration.*

**MAUD**

Nice dress.

**EV**

I just got the cardboard.

> *She flips it over and sets it down. It will do.*

**MAUD**

Could you just get me out, just one of these?

> *She lifts the little tin of aspirin.*

**EV**

You want a whole one?

**MAUD**

Please.

> *He allocates one tablet. He snaps the tin and pockets it. A cup of*
> *water to Maud from the reservoir. He returns to the stove and the*
> *herring. To dark. The sound of a Jimmy Rodgers TB blues.*

**EV**

You could paint a board of Bill and Beauty. Now there was a pair.

> *A brief flare from the lamp. Maud works away in her little corner.*
> *She tilts the mirror behind the lamp. She bends above the board*
> *and tray. The brush darts in and out of the tins like a swallow on*
> *a cliff above the river. It darts down to the picture.*

> *In darkness.*

**EV**

What are you colouring?

**MAUD**
Bluebirds on the nest, a fall of snow.

**EV**
May the Lord save us.

## ACT ONE SCENE FIVE

# BIG JUNIOR OFFERS A WINTER'S WOOD

*The light is alike The Potato Eaters. Ev's plate is cracked. He lifts the plate to the dripping. He sops it up with bread. He highgrades a slice of bread, checks his teeth with a finger, and passes the crusts, one after the other, to Maud. They eat in silence.*

**EV**
Look out for bones.

*From pleasant quiet to pleasant sound: Oxbells in the evening. A knock on the door. Ev lifts his head.*

**MAUD**
I don't know.

*Ev does a softshoe shuffle. To the door. He listens. He flinches at a rap. He recovers. He peeks out the window. Startled, he turns to dump their dinners to the pot. He whispers.*

**EV**
Big Junior.

*Ev returns to the door and bar. He slips the latches. Hooks off eyes and the door opens. Junior in good humour to the sill. Ev stands at the entrance.*

**BIG JUNIOR**
Good Evening, Ev.

**EV**
Good evenin.

*Junior peeks around him.*

**BIG JUNIOR**
Why, there you are: Good Evening Maud.

**EV**
Good Evening then.

*Ev tries to shut the door but Junior gets a foot in.*

**BIG JUNIOR**
We're on our ways back home for dinner. If that's what got you worried.

**MAUD**
Come in, Junior!

*Ev gives way.*
**EV**
Don't let the heat out.

*Junior's big boots look like buckets on his feet. The boots are precisely laced and tied. His clothes are neat and organized. His shirt is a red-black check and buttoned up. A whip on his belt, a cross at his throat. An all-embracing smile.*

**BIG JUNIOR**
I hope the evening finds the Missus well?

**EV**
She's tired out.

**MAUD**
I'm tired, Junior. But come on in. Now Junior, how's Pearline?

**BIG JUNIOR**
A-one. Thank you. Baking for tomorrow.

*To Ev. Relax. Relax. Not here for a collection.*

**MAUD**
Tell Pearline that we're still eating off that loaf.

**BIG JUNIOR**
Why! Weren't no good?

*He laughs.*

**MAUD**
No, No! No. Her bread's so good. We've been saving it.

*Maud approaches Junior. She looks to the Road for Little Juny.*

**BIG JUNIOR**
Juny took the team on up the lane.

**MAUD**
Such a good boy.

**EV**
He'll end up in the Poor Farm.

**MAUD**
Oh!

**EV**
Well, he got fired from the boats.

>    *Junior turns to take Ev's measure.*

**MAUD**
He never.

**EV**
Yes he did!

>    *Junior addresses Everett. For a loaded moment, it is as if these
>    two were all the world.*

**BIG JUNIOR**
Juny did the work of two. Loading that boat. The Harbour Master
would not pay him what he paid the Digby boys. Juny throwed him
in the Harbour. That lucky man. The tide was in.

>    *He smiles.*

And then he helped the man on out.

>    *A chance for an apology. Ev does not take it.*

You put Juny on a gang, he'll do the work a two. Ev. Now. No son
of mine will need to be looked after. The flesh will come rate off my
fingers first.

>    *Junior to good humour. To Maud.*

He'll find a girl, and then he'll settle down.

**MAUD**
He's the kind of young man got the whole world hoping.

**BIG JUNIOR**
Ain't his fault he's so good looking.

*Maud laughs.*

Ev. Me and Juny are going back on up the Ridge. We came by to ask. If you'd go shares. Go shares on the hardwood. And you can have the scrub.

*Ev cannot meet Big Junior's eyes.*

First light.
*Ev thinks.*

**MAUD**
Ev.

**EV**
Well, I can't say. I got a lot to do.

*The revelation of a great secret.*

Winter coming on. I got a lot to do.

**BIG JUNIOR**
We cut four cords. It's good and dry.

**EV**
Dry?

**BIG JUNIOR**
We felled the ash last winter. The birch in July. Snap, crackle, pop!

*Ev evades.*

We can bring the stovewood down tomorrow. Then when it snows we'll bolt the runners to the sledge. One cold night, the Ridge will freeze up slick. And we'll go get the logs. You can ride up on the sledge.

*He smiles.*

And down the hill will go a whole lot faster.

**EV**
Oh I don't know. And where you say you're cutting?

**BIG JUNIOR**
This side of the Ridge. By Old John Ayer's.

**EV**
Asylum Road? The Judge has got the deed on that.

**BIG JUNIOR**
The Judge said we should go ahead, and thin it out a little.

**EV**
Thin it out! Yeah, thin it out. A lot of people thinning out the Ridge.
Why I seen Nate up there a resting in the light of an August clearing.

*Ev shakes his head.*

The Judge don't go way back up there, don't know how thin it's
getting.

**BIG JUNIOR**
Oh, maybe he does. Maybe he does. Do not shut your hand against
your brother. Lend him sufficient for his need.

**EV**
Is that from the Bible?

**BIG JUNIOR**
I hope so.

**EV**
That's enough of that.

*Junior is tested, but accepts the harm.*

**BIG JUNIOR**
Two shares. Let's call it. Limbed and trimmed. We'll buck it up and
you can stack.

**EV**
I ain't the man I used to be.

**MAUD**
It would be good, to get that wood. In case the winter was hard.

*Ev turns from Junior to face Maud. He turns from Maud to face
Junior.*

**BIG JUNIOR**
Steady on.

*Ev avoids a helpful hand.*

**EV**
I drop one and I'm done for. Maybe you could bring the stovewood
by.

**BIG JUNIOR**
I just thought that you could use that hardwood. We could use a
third man on the haul.

**EV**
I got a load a slabwood coming. From the mill.

*Junior winks to Maud and turns to go.*

**BIG JUNIOR**
From the mill. You must be doing well.

**MAUD**
Two sold today.

*Ev panics. He hisses for silence. Junior laughs at Everett's
secrecy.*

**BIG JUNIOR**
Maud, Maud, that's good to hear. Good work, my dear, is the light of
the world.

*Ev to the door.*

**EV**
Don't let us keep you in the dark.

*Ev opens the door. Juny appears in the doorway. Startled, Ev
jumps like a pheasant out of the field. Juny, calmly, waits out the
foolishness.*

**JUNY**
Evening all.

*Juny steps in.*

**EV**
What are you feeding him.

*Juny: to his father.*

**JUNY**
I left Bright and Lion by the brook. Lion will look after Bright.

*Big Junior nods. Juny bows to Maud. Ev throws up his hands.*

**MAUD**

Juny, you have rose up like a weed. Some lucky girl is going to eat you up!

**JUNY**

Mum says to tell you if I saw you: You could come along. She'll do your hair.

**EV**

I'll let you know.

*Junior laughs.*

**JUNY**

I think Mum meant, <u>her</u> hair. I mean to say, Mum hopes she might come over while the men are off to work.

*Alert, Junior steps in.*

**BIG JUNIOR**

Maud. Come Sunday we'll be singing the old, old songs. I know you love them so.

*Ev shakes his head.*

**MAUD**

I guess not.

**EV**

It's a long walk down to there. For her.

**BIG JUNIOR**

Braddy's daddy got a car.

*Maud looks to Ev.*

The Choir is coming along quite well. Come Sunday, Juny's singing O, Abide With Me.

**MAUD**

Abide With Me. My favourite.

**JUNY**

Me too. O Abide With Me.

*Juny holds Maud's hands.*

Well. If you're feeling better.

> *Ev can hardly believe his eyes. Maud forgets her hands and smiles to Little Juny.*

**BIG JUNY and JUNY and MAUD**

We're going then. Evening then. Evening Maud. See yah.

> *Ev nods but does not speak. Juny and Junior exit. The door shuts. The bar and locks and latches. The sound of a solo violin against a dust of snow. Maud imagines the wild ride down the Ridge. In darkness.*

**EV**
I got to take the handle off the outside of that door.

## ACT ONE SCENE SIX

# GRAVES OPEN, GHOSTS ESCAPE LIKE WHISPERS AND FEARFUL SECRETS VISIT

*Ox bells sound, resound and fade.*

**EV**
As if we'd go to a coloured church.

**MAUD**
I <u>would</u> like. Just once, to hear Little Juny sing.

*No response.*

My mother's family was Baptist.

**EV**
They wasn't coloured, was they?

*She ignores him.*

**MAUD**
I've heard him singing Danny Boy. Along the Lane. Sound like chimes. He <u>does</u> have a lovely voice.

*Ev scrapes a meal from the pot. The top off a tall tin.*
**EV**
I'm looking for a cracker.

**MAUD**
Just biscuit.

*Ev taps a tooth.*

**EV**
Can't risk it.

**MAUD**
The Judge might bring us a box of crackers.

**EV**

Anyways, I heard them in the summer. When the door was open to the whole, wide world. It's not the same.

**MAUD**

Sure it is. It's the same. When other helpers, fail, and comforts flee.

> *Ev returns the cracker tin to the cracker box shelf. He bends over Maud and shakes his head. He sits to eat. Swoop fork and knifery. Maud sits quietly with folded hands.*

**MAUD**

Cut out the church. Cut out the neighbours. I'm going to end up talking to the birds.

> *Hesitant.*

If I can't go to hear a Christmas hymn, it seems just like. The year was all for nothing.

**EV**

Bone!

> *He spits.*

**MAUD**

Clara asks me over every year. The shade on the verandah. The strawberries were good this year. Not once since we been here. I never crossed that road. What must they think?

> *Ev points.*

**EV**

What's over there we ain't got here? There's a woman, ten dollar day and then she gets upset. A man will take it in his stride.

> *Maud examines her hands. As if she can't believe what has become of them.*

**MAUD**

How many times they sent a meal across? A pie plate and wax paper. Send the child along some little thing.

**EV**

See. That's the thing. If you start going over there, they won't send food across.

**MAUD**

I look over there and watch the child at play. Stop and look across the Road.
What must she think of me?

**EV**

I see what's bothering you.

*He raises an accusatory finger.*

We had a deal. We said. And you and me agreed. That's all in the past. We said and now you want to break the deal.

**MAUD**

I'm talking about the neighbour child.

*He points.*

**EV**

That's what you're saying now.

*A glance to the Road.*

That one. Should be grateful. Was took in.

**MAUD**

Not too many from the Farm took in.

*Silence. What child does she remember? Ev to the window to lower the blind. He returns to his meal. It defeats him.*

**EV**

I had nothing to do with that. They tell to me, to dig a grave. I dug a grave. What Jinky said for me to do, I done. That's that, that's all, and that's the end of it. And you're the one to talk.

*Ev is in a fearful world. He turns accusatory.*

I never had no wanton child. I kept to my part of the deal. You're best off to forget all that.

**MAUD**

No christening, dead, and not one Christian letter.

**EV**

At least a Poor Farm child. Each one of them, they got a silver ring. They got a silver ring when they was buried.

*Maud winces.*

You brought it up! Some day! Jinky got to pay. Some never lasted but a single night. A moth live longer.

**EV**
You should hear what the Bible says a child born out a wedlock. Oh, I got the prophets in my head. Jink used to read to the dummies. Sunday breakfast. Jink. Keeper. Master. Got more gold than anyone a ever dream of.

**MAUD**
He's lasted.

**EV**
Maybe in the crawl space, maybe. Got a lock on it.

> *He thinks.*

I don't know. Somewheres he got a forty pound stone-a-gold.

> *To himself.*

All those nights of walking, I couldn't find it.

> *To Maud.*

What's done is done. You do the Cats and get that done. We need the cash for kerosene.

> *Ev takes wooden slats and a hammer from the Cabinet. He shuts the Cabinet. To the window looking out to the Farm. He nails the slats.*

**MAUD**
You nailing up that window?

**EV**
I ain't got on my hands what Jink got coming.

> *She starts with each fall of the hammer. Ev returns the hammer to the cabinet. The lock.*

**MAUD**
People still bring flowers. Lay them by the fieldstone wall.

**EV**
The fieldstone wall. There you go.

**MAUD**

I wasn't speaking a the child.

**EV**

I know what child. I knew then. I know now. Stick to my word. I'm just careful what I say. And you said yes. I kept my word and here you are. You say yes and then you go rate back. Forget.

**MAUD**

I haven't. Forgotten anything.

*She fixes him with the truth of a measured stare.*

**EV**

It's dangerous to even speak. I'm lucky Mother got me out. It's all in here. I sleep with that.
*A forefinger to drill his skull.*

They never made no more like her.

**MAUD**

I know what I lost.

**EV**

That's enough.

**MAUD**

I sit here working. By myself. I sit here still. Not just remembering. I still got hopes. The coloured. They're good to one another. When we were young, the coloured come on round. Father gavem silver dimes for Christmas. Quiet as a photograph. And sing. Away in a manger. No crib for a bed. Junior offers a winter's wood. What do we do? Christmas morning, hear them from the hollow. Silent night.

**EV**

I like a silent night myself.

*Ev retreats. He wanders about. The dishes and a bucket. Now and then he looks to Maud. Maud prepares to settle to her corner. She struggles with the lamp and mirror. A board.*

**MAUD**

The whole world knows that they're not wanted here.

**EV**

Don't slip off. You're just upset. On account of Junior. Junior! Not one soul in that dark shaking church could buy a share in a little tin wheelbarrow. I'm going to church the one last time. And it won't be where that deacon spouts his head off.

*He brings to Maud a cup of tea. One for himself. A sip. The dishes and the cleaning up.*

Anyways tomorrow. I got to go down to the weir.

*Maud looks up.*

They'll leave all kinds a mackerel. That's why I couldn't go with Junior for the wood. Tonight, I'm going to get some more of them husks. We got to feed the last two hens we got.

**MAUD**
Don't get caught.

*He continues with the dishes. He turns up her lamp.*

**EV**
You didn't get much done today. All that song and dance.

*A nod.*

You could paint Big Junior's team. The Judge would take that in a wink.

**MAUD**
He wants the Cats.

**EV**
What for? The Cats?

*She nods. A terrible thought alights. A whisper.*

The Cats! You scraped them off!

*She nods to the wall.*

**MAUD**
Oh no. I saved them. I just got to add more blossoms to the Heaven.

*Ev subsides. He delivers the Cats to her corner. She works away.*

**EV**
You better get it done. I got to watch the things you do. A lot of secrets, for a little house. I'm asking him ten dollars.

**MAUD**
Ev.

**EV**
Not one word. If it was up to you, your father dead, your mother dead. You'd be sleeping in a steel cot on the topmost floor.

> *He waves to the nailed-up window. Across the Field to the Poor Farm.*

You'd fit in fine. I'm asking ten. He got it.

**MAUD**
He brings half of what we eat.

> *He taps the Cats.*

**EV**
The first we started. I never thought this stuff would sell. But we fooled them.

> *To the cracker tin.*

Let me ask you something serious. Have you been feeding crackers to the birds?

> *He turns the tin upside down. He licks the dust on his finger.*

**MAUD**
No.

**EV**
Cause they're leaving. And we're staying. Last time the Judge was here, how <u>are</u> we off for crackers and you said good.

**MAUD**
I was embarassed.

**EV**
What?

**MAUD**
He brought so much. All those tins a peaches. I was embarassed.

**EV**
When the Judge comes, you tell him we ain't got nuthin. Nuthin.

Tell him we're starving. No! When he asts. Wait. No. Don't tell him anything. Just nod your head.

*Maud nods her head.*

For the Love of the Days Gone By. Junior took the Judge six cord a wood last winter. Every single, walloping Christmas the Peach Man hauls four barrels of those apples down to the Judge's cellar. Half the time they rot and Juny got to haul them out. Know what he done? He sent two barrels to the coloureds on the Buchan Road.

*He sips his tea in triumph. She works at the Cats.*

**MAUD**
It's hard to ask. He is so generous.

**EV**
Generous! That ain't generous! Naw-thin! Not one hungry, hobo thing! Generous! I don't call that generous! I don't call that generous a-tall. Lost Waste is what it is.

**MAUD**
That first year Junior came, the Judge brought stuff, all winter long.

**EV**
He thinks he's buying his salvation. That ain't generous. It's religious.

**MAUD**
The Judge ain't religious. He's Salvation Army.

*He spits out a sip of tea. Aggravated, he pours his tea back into the pot.*

**EV**
That's it! Can't drink it!

*A final splash of tea for emphasis.*

That's it for me no more I'm done! First you couldn't let me eat. And now my cup of tea.

*He sticks the dishes in the galvanized bucket. He lifts his boots up to the warming oven of the stove. He blows out one lamp and turns down the second.*

**EV**

I'm going out again when the moon comes up. Get them cornhusks for the chickens.

**MAUD**

I'll need the light until I'm done.

> *Ev turns the dampers down and scuttles ashes over the coals. He strips his shirt, sniffs the air and hangs the shirt on a nail behind the stove. He climbs the ladder.*
>
> *A careful glance to the loft and Maud turns up the lamp for light. A careful glance and she opens the drafts to the firebox. She kneads her fingers and sits to paint the blossoms of a heaven.*
>
> *A shout from the dark of the loft.*

**EV**

Generous!

> *Maud starts. And recovers. She dabs the board with her apron to fix an errant drop. She looks up to wonder if he might start up again. The radio plays of its own volition and selection. She picks up a brush and starts again.*

**MAUD**

Well, I think you are the prettiest little kittens. The two of you. And you have a very pretty mother. I should say, the best of mothers.

> *She paints.*

I can see you favour her.

> *She paints.*

The prettiest kittens in Heaven. And I would say she misses you. Do you miss her?

> *The Cats is done. A struggle to pick it up. To walk. She props The Three Black Cats up on the warming oven. An effort. The stovelights sparkle about the Cats.*
>
> *She blows out the lamp. She closes the dampers to the cast-iron stove.*
> *She struggles to ascend the stairs. The stairs are steep and not much of a rail. To dark. The Three Black Cats.*

## ACT ONE SCENE SEVEN

# THE JUDGE OF THE WEALTH OF THE WORLD

*Morning light. Maud descends. Straight to the warming oven for the Cats. A critical appraisal. She nods.*

*She replaces the Cats to the warming oven, takes a cracker from her apron, listens for Ev and steps to the step to crumble the cracker. She sits in her corner and takes up the cardboard from behind her chair. She dips a brush in brown. Ev descends, leaning and ducking, down the stairs. He sniffs the air.*

**EV**
Every dog in Marshalltown was out last night.

*He nods. He sniffs.*

**MAUD**
The Cats are done.

**EV**
Ah!

*He rattles irons and blows on the coals.*

You know what you never painted? Junior's team. They got First Prize at the Weymouth Fair.

*She looks at her board, laughs, and places it aside. And limps to her shoes by the stove.*

That dagon from Arth Robinson. With Lion. Lion and Bright. What a strong-looking team.

*Maud has trouble with the intricate loops of the laces.*

You seen them ever time he goes up on the Ridge.

**MAUD**
I never saw them, in their brasses.

*Defeated by the laces.*

You never took me to the Fair.

**EV**
Never?

> *She nods.*

You want some help there with your shoes?

**MAUD**
I just can't seem to get my fingers down around.

**EV**
Not any worse?

> *She twists and rubs her hands. Ev, kindly, tenderly, expertly ties the laces.*

**MAUD**
Just a cold morning.

> *Ev rises to examine the Cats. He nicks the picture with a fingernail.*

**EV**
It's dry.

> *He turns, as if to say that she has done the job.*

Strange. I knew a cat like that.

> *He twists his head this way and that.*

Cat like that, a long, long time ago. What do you want for breakfast?

> *Bread in a frying pan. The Cats attracts.*

**MAUD**
I'll take some tea, please, with the bread.

> *She looks out the window.*

I hope we get this sun all day.

> *Ev breaks to the Cats. A puzzle. A hand up to speak, then silent.*

They're just dreams. I guess them up.

**EV**
Yesterday was just too much. One shock after another.

> *A visitation.*

We can sell this one.

*This pleases Maud.*

I'm going out and look for an egg.

**MAUD**
I ain't going nowheres.

*Ev smiles at the joke and exits. The chickens squawk. Ev returns
with an egg in each hand.*
**EV**
Holy O Lifting. Look at this. No eggs for days. And. Each a egg! It
was them husks. A lot of corn still on them husks. I could hear them
pecking half the night.

*He's happy to emphasize his point.*

**MAUD**
Where exactly did you get those husks?

**EV**
Those hens, just peck away on husks. That's why the yolks so
yellow. I got the best part of a sack.

**MAUD**
Yes. But where did you get those husks.

*Ev is reluctant to answer.*

**EV**
Full on the dump!

*Irritated.*

I'm not the only man that tends the Poor Farm dump. You should
see what they don't use up.

*A silence.*

I never went into the Field. The dogs were following and right up to
the fence. And then I took a spill. Lost some. Maybe I'll go get them.

**MAUD**
Olive said, that if we needed anything. All we had to do was ask.

*This nettles Ev.*

**EV**
Well I ain't going to beg.

**MAUD**
I just don't want. The Sheriff showing up.

*Both Maud and Ev look to the door. Ev stares, and quietly he nods. The bread. The tea. A motor interrupts.*

**EV**
The Judge! Big Black Chrysler. V-8 motor. And a running board like a gold-almighty hearse.

*Ev unbars the door. He grabs a hat from a peg and skips outside. The dog barks from the back. To the yard.*

*Maud waits on the step. The Judge enters backwards. He turns. The revelations of his baskets and a rose.*

Good Morning, Your Honour!

*Ev doffs his hat and holds it. The Judge advances to Maud on the step.*

**THE JUDGE**
Tis the last rose of summer, left blooming alone. All her lovely companions, are faded and gone.

*It takes two hands for Maud to take the rose. The rose to her nose.*

**MAUD**
A primrose. Smells so sweet.

**THE JUDGE**
Maud, my girl, I brought you some of the world's finest cheese. A little Stilton. You like cheese, I take it?

*Ev steps behind the judge and nods his head to Maud.*

**EV**
She dotes on it.

*The Judge explains each parcel. Some are wrapped in butcher paper, some in newspaper. Ev contorts to see what next the Judge has brought.*

**EV**
She don't like that cheese that got the rot in it.

**THE JUDGE**
And here's a little bit of Cheddar.

> *A two pound wedge.*

**EV**
That's what she likes!

**THE JUDGE**
This Stilton. Is the same the Queen takes with her tea. This day, there will be you, Maud Lewis, and our Queen Elizabeth, with Stilton for their tea.

> *Maud accepts the Stilton and the Cheddar.*

I do relish it myself.

> *The Judge ignores Everett's twists. He breaks off a bit of cheddar.*

Just wait! Try that. The finest cheese in all the world.

> *Maud nibbles. The Judge nibbles. Everett all but salivates.*

**EV**
That kind of cheese. She rel-ishes.

> *The plenty of the parcels are a problem. She laughs.*

**MAUD**
You're loading me rate up.

> *Ev tries to get the cheese. Ev is foiled by the bulk of the Judge.*

**THE JUDGE**
But you, absolutely, must promise me to keep it cool.

**EV**
We'll drop it in the bucket down the well.

**THE JUDGE**
You like sausages?

**EV**
Does she ever!

> *Great nods to Maud.*

**THE JUDGE**
New potatoes?

**EV**
Just look at them!

> *Nose in a bag.*

**THE JUDGE**
And some peas. And a bag a pole beans. Do you make a hodge-podge?

> *Maud accumulates.*

Cream and peas on the potatoes. Salt and pepper. Butter just the size of an egg.

> *Maud to interior with goods.*

**EV**
She just loves cooking. But she runs out.

> *Maud returns to get a pie. She turns to take it in. The Judge stops Ev with a tin of sardines.*

**THE JUDGE**
Black's Harbour. The Best Sardines that Money Can Buy. The Prince of Norway. Just imagine.

> *The Judge compares his visage in the window to the Prince.*

Good looking man.

> *Maud returns. He hands her a paper bag of onions. In the House and out.*

Could you use a flat of eggs?

**MAUD**
Oh! No! Just this morning.

> *She points to the coop. Ev interrupts.*

**EV**
Can't remember what a real egg looks like!

> *And shakes his head to Maud.*

Ar hens are dying one by one. It's weasels.

**THE JUDGE**
They eggs are on the back seat. I'll go get them.

> *The Judge strides off to fetch the eggs. Ev gives instruction in the art of nodding.*

**EV**
Holy Rolling Ezekiel Maud. Help me out a little.

**MAUD**
I thought. There was something wrong there with your neck.

> *Everett warns Maud with a raised finger. The Judge returns with a flat of eggs. He dangles an onion bag of tins of Carnation Evaporated Milk. He balances boxes of crackers. Maud sits aside on a willow-twig bench. He places the gifts about the bench.*

**THE JUDGE**
I brought you a dozen evaporated milk.

> *Ev nods. Maud nods.*

Crackers?

> *Maud, exactly three times, nods.*

**EV**
The poor thing was just saying! She wished, she wished she had a cracker and what a pity some nights all she does is dream about a big box a salteens.

> *The Judge laughs.*

**THE JUDGE**
You'd better take them in.

> *Ev takes the bounty to the jumble of bread boxes.*

**MAUD**
Judge, you're better than a store.

> *Maud tries to stand. The Judge espies fragility.*

**THE JUDGE**
How are you then?

**MAUD**

Oh I'm alright. I stayed up late. The Cats is done.

> *The pride of the finish of a work of art.*

I'll get it.

> *She attempts to stand. She falls back to the bench.*

Well! What was that!

> *The Judge assists. She rests a breath. She gains her balance with touches to the House. She returns with the Cats and props it up on the storm door. Ev opens and closes the bread boxes and stuffs the victuals in. He sees Maud with the Cats and follows.*

**EV**

I told her. Nobody on this road would want those cats!

> *The Judge lifts the Cats off the battens of the door.*

**THE JUDGE**

My oh my. My goodness.

> *Maud is embarassed.*

**MAUD**

Your Honour.

**THE JUDGE**

Your goodness!

> *They laugh.*

**EV**

You could put a ox in! Rate down there.

> *Ev taps the board. The Judge is offended.*

**THE JUDGE**

I'm giving this one to my little girl. I'll be dead and buried and she will love it still.

**EV**

Oh, a little girl might like it.

**THE JUDGE**

Maud, it is a jewel.

*Intrigue.*

Here, what is that shadow.

*Surprised.*

**MAUD**
I couldn't tell you! I guess. It's just a shadow from the trees.

**THE JUDGE**
By the fallen blossoms. Long there in the grass. It looks like the shadow of my little girl.

**MAUD**
The shadow of a someone, come along to play with her.

*A quiet joke. A smile.*

**THE JUDGE**
Good then. What do I owe you?

**EV**
Oh for that, well I need ten. I got to have it.

**MAUD**
He don't mean the half of what he says.

**EV**
Hey now.

*The Judge adopts a patient smile.*

**THE JUDGE**
Everett. Keep quiet.

*Ev steps back. As if being sentenced, he folds his hands.*

**MAUD**

We just hope your daughter likes it. That's all.

*Everett nods.*

What I liked when I was a little girl. And you said how she lost her kitten.

**THE JUDGE**
That's the price you pay for living on the Road. She liked Blackie. Look how Blackie's coat shows up against the blossoms.

*Maud takes up the rose from her apron.*

**MAUD**
What's your little girl like?

**THE JUDGE**
What does she like?

*Maud laughs.*

**MAUD**
No. Who does she favour?

**THE JUDGE**
Rosina, takes after her mother's family, the Watsons.

**MAUD**
Rosina. You don't hear that name too much these days.

*The conversation exasperates Ev. Where's the money?*

**THE JUDGE**
She started off "Rosina." Now she likes the sound of "Rose." A good child. She is thoughtful. She remembers. When you are absent, she remembers.

**MAUD**
Kind.

*The Judge replaces the Cats to the door. He takes a clip of cash from his pocket. Ev is transfixed.*

**THE JUDGE**
That she is.

**MAUD**
I'm happy Rose will have the Cats.

*She does not want the money. Her hands to her apron.*

**THE JUDGE**
Come now, Maud. Let's not the world, hear you and I quarrel. Let us pay you a little something.

*Ev nods, and waits for Maud to nod.*

**MAUD**
We've been friends a long time. Judge. And I never give you nothing.

**EV**
Judge, women are no good at this.

*A glance to Ev to reprimand. Ev bows his head.*

**THE JUDGE**
Ev.

**EV**
Yes.

**THE JUDGE**
Would you be good enough to go and fix for me a bit a that cheddar?

*Ev peeks with one eye.*
**EV**
Now!

**THE JUDGE**
If you could.

*Ev to the interior*

On a cracker would be good.

*The Judge attempts to fold two bills into Maud's hands. She turns and closes her awkward hands. He tucks the cash into her apron pocket. It's the apron with the heart on the pocket, the same as may be seen on the door. Ev returns and proffers the cheese. The Judge espies Ev's hands. He takes the cracker by a corner and drops it into a basket.*

**MAUD**
Judge.

*Hand to her apron. The other, the rose.*

**THE JUDGE**
Let me tell you something, Maud. I been bringing you some money. Don't mean nothing compared to this.

*The painting from the battens of the door.*

It's like the sun that strikes the pebbles in the brook. Everything you paint is lit up just like life. People come right up the drive and past the aspen, ring bell on ar front door and try to buy these off me. Can't bring myself to let one go.

*He shows the Cats to Ev. Ev raises a hand, and lets it fall.*

Every oncet a while, we take up strings. And we string those strings up to the rafters in the dining room, take out your paintings and we hang them up. Forty or so it looks like a stained glass window. Everything I'm starting to miss, I find in what you do. In the afternoon, and later on, when the light comes off the river. And hits the works of them, well Mister Man!

**MAUD**
Oh, I would like to see that.

*This embarasses. She retreats.*

I'm starting now to miss things too.

*The Judge gives Maud a little squeeze on her arm.*

Judge.
*A little smile.*

And there's things I know I'll never have. And I thank you, because the way you talk it's just as good.

*He considers.*

**THE JUDGE**
It's better.

*And it may well be.*

Your voice worries me.

**MAUD**
I've been having something in my chest.

**THE JUDGE**
You better help yourself to a piece a that pie. You never know, it might be the walking pneumonia. That's what I do when I'm poorly. I stuff myself.

*A sigh. He breaks into a fragment of song.*

So long it's been good to know yah, But I got to be getting along. Don't be too hard on Ev, now.

*They laugh.*

**MAUD**
No, Judge. I won't.

> *The Judge slips his baskets to an arm. The Cats up with the
> other.*

**THE JUDGE**
Tell you what. Ice cream! I'll stop at the store and bring you some.
I woke up in the night with the thought of a great big feed of clams.
You can only get those quohogs in Meteghan. I'll stop by Andy
Perry's, get some ice cream.

> *The Judge to the Chrysler.*

**EV**
Wait! Wait! What about the painting?

**THE JUDGE**
I have it here. I thank-yah.

> *The Judge stops on the path. From a distance, he turns.*

Ev, you still got two doors there on your outhouse?

> *Ev doesn't quite understand.*

**EV**
There's two holes.

> *The Judge laughs. He whistles a phrase to the chickadees on the
> red brick chimney. He tosses the cracker from the basket. And
> away.*

**EV**
If that don't take the cake. The Judge made off with it.

**MAUD**
Now now.

**EV**
The Judge! Broad daylight stole my board what I got off the dump.

**MAUD**
Oh no.

**EV**
That's what I call it. Break and enter.

> *A swinging arm.*

**MAUD**
Hold on to this.

> *She passes the rose to Everett. She searches for the bills. The rattle and motor of the Chrysler leaving. A toot. She waves.*

**EV**
A dusty old rose. A evening rose. A pale little petal from out the ditch.

> *Despair.*

**MAUD**
Don't get beside yourself. Give me a second.

> *She tries to hook the bills in her pocket. The cash falls from the apron to the millwheel step. Ev espies the bills. Stops. Stunned. Darts to the bills. He drops the rose.*

**EV**
Two fi-i-ives.

> *Discovery gives way to suspicion.*

How come he give them bills to you!

**MAUD**
I didn't ask him to.

**EV**
What!

**MAUD**
From the day my father died, I never asked a man. For anything.

> *The hope which came with the sun is gone. She tries to scramble up the rose, but her hands will not allow. Ev watches but does not assist.*

**MAUD**
Help me.

**EV**
What.

**MAUD**
Help me, Everett.

*As sudden as a shifting wind.*

**EV**
A course! A course!

*He picks up the rose. He helps Maud to the bench beside the
step. They sit.*

**MAUD**
Sit a minute. All that rimrack wears me out.

*Ev returns the rose.*

**EV**
We'll store the most of that. A good haul. The cheese will store. The
sardines they'll be just as good in March. I once kept a tin a milk
three years. I opened it. It was alive. You keep a cracker dry, it lasts
damn near a year.

*She doesn't reply.*

The Judge is a ag-gravating soul. Some people get a little too high.
Handing out. Telling you what. A little too high.

*No reply.*

I remember when his mother worked along the Cross. She used to go
the store with German money. Look, are you listening?

*The light to Black and White. Big Junior and Bert appear in light.
A wandering brevity in the discretion of the Director. They watch
Everett lean toward Maud but the words cannot be heard.*

**BIG JUNIOR**
Everett Lewis. There was a character out of the parables.

**BERT**
He was as crooked a man as ever stumbled on the road. Crooked as
a knot and burl. Mean as frost.

**BIG JUNIOR**
Let's not judge. Lest we be judged. If Maud meant anything to us,
that's what it was. Look for the best in everyone.

What we could be.

*Big Junior believes he sees Little Juny in the distance and maybe
he does and raises his hand, but the apparition vanishes before
him. He is astonished. A momentary hope and terror.*

That boy looked like Juny.

**BERT**

Junior. Juny's been gone a long, long time.

*To light and colour.*

**MAUD**

I can't listen all the time. Yes, I'm listening.

*He measures her regard for the rose.*

I was just remembering. The day I came.

**EV**

Well, nothing's changed. If I knowed that you liked roses. What are you remembering now!

*Accepting quiet, she looks to her partner.*

**MAUD**

I was just remembering you.

*He starts, as if he has an answer, then subsides.*

**EV**

Remember me. Everybody on the road knows me.

**MAUD**

Yes, they do.

**EV**

Is anybody going to remember you?

*She laughs. A settling of his limbs. Maud holds the rose up to the light. She turns the rose about to see its curls and colours. She places the rose in a crack in the windowsill. Within the window decorations, it looks like it belongs. She kneads her hands.*

*She reaches out to touch him but he places the cash in his chest pocket and buttons up the pocket and pats it. He folds his arms across his chest. All the sadness of the world is locked up in her smile. She closes her hands and hides them in the folds of her linen apron.*

*The radio and a Jimmy Rodgers tune: Rock All Your Babies to Sleep.*

## ACT TWO SCENE ONE

# THE SERMON TO THE ASH

*Passing shadows and sun. The day becomes warm. Ev stands.
Off with his shirt. The revelation of his woollen underwear. The
transfer of cash to the chain and wallet.*

**MAUD**
Indian summer.

*She crumbles crackers to the sill, and looks about. The
chickadees have been absent for two days.*

**EV**
The clam shells were a bad idea. I'll turn them over.

**MAUD**
Well they didn't cost us much.

*Ev lifts a rake from a nail on the House. He rakes the path. He
sniffs the shells.*

**EV**
Should a run a bucket on-em now and then.

*She wets an apron tip with her tongue.*

**MAUD**
Well the well was low all summer.

*Peace. She cleans specks of paint from her arm and apron. He
places his boots on the step and returns to the seat.*

**EV**
Sit still, will yah.

**MAUD**
I'm giving you room.

**EV**
Just be care-full. You break your arm, we're done for.

*She smiles.*

In my life, I never had a pair a brand-new boots. What was you
painting deep into the other night?

**MAUD**
I'll show you.

*She sighs.*

Not too.
*She takes a breath.*

Many more days like this. The sun feels good on my old bones.

**EV**
For the winter, I can move your chair to over by the stove.

**MAUD**
I like the corner. Watch the world go by.

*A single, ringing gospel bell.*

**EV**
That's the Anglicans. They're first. They're some early. That's all I got to say.

*He sighs.*

Some glad I'm not an Anglican. Who was that went up the Ridge?

**MAUD**
The Potters.

*A motor. It fades.*

**EV**
When did she say she's coming back?

*Hand to the sun.*

**MAUD**
She didn't say.

*The sound of a single ox bell. Ev swivels to the ring.*
**EV**
That was ox-bells in the lane. Hear that?

*She nods.*

You see then. I was right.

**MAUD**
It's Sunday. Can't be Junior.

**EV**
Got to be. Only a fool would work an ox in this kind a heat.

> *Swivel ears.*

It's strange, how quick a ox will die. On its knees and roll rate over. Just from standing in the sun.

**MAUD**
Ev. Be good. If it's Junior, you be good.

**EV**
That's why they're coming up around. They're stopping at the pond. Two oxen. They'll break down the bank.

**MAUD**
Let them get water. After all.

> *Ev stands. The bench of willow branches tips. Maud nearly goes over, but a hand to the rainpipe.*

**EV**
Get those beasts out a my pond! You break down the bank!

> *The bells loud, a tin-brass country melody.*

**BIG JUNIOR**
Gee Bright Gee! Whoa up there Lion! Catch hold Juny!

**JUNY**
I got him!

> *Ev watches something amazing. He turns to Maud, did she see that? Big Junior to the yard with his whip and dressed for church. Ev slips on his boots, his laces loose.*

**BIG JUNIOR**
They'll stand there in the rushes. They like the cool of the water on their cloven hoof.

**EV**
I didn't know that that was you.

**BIG JUNIOR**
You won't begrudge cool water to the beasts of the field. They're gathering winter fu-el.

*Laughs at himself as Wenceslaus.*

**MAUD**

I'll get you a cup, Junior

*She fetches a ladle.*

**BIG JUNIOR**

Most apprec-a-tive, Mrs. Lewis.

*Ev draws a bucket from the well. Junior takes a drink of water. Juny fires the wood across the lane. A stick too close to the kennel. The dog barks sharply. Maud is affronted by the manners of the dog.*

**EV**

Don't fire it onto the shed!

**BIG JUNIOR**

Don't yell at Juny, Ev, he's not an ox.

*Junior takes a drink of water to Juny. Maud inspects the wood.*

**MAUD**

Why it's all sawn and split!

*Juny passes, wood piled up against his chest. Ev examines his acquisition. Treasure and greed.*

**EV**

Ash and maple and apple! Fine, fine wood.

**BIG JUNIOR**

We cleaned up that old orchard. Juny cut the each and every stick. The wood there is a apple struck by lightning. That wood will burn as sweet as the promise of the life hereafter. When Pearline wants to bake a pie, I load the stove with apple.

**MAUD**

Juny done a fine, fine job.

**BIG JUNIOR**

There's nothing Juny cannot do. He read before he went to school.

*Juny with a load of wood.*

I do admit that I have prayed.

*He looks at his wonderful son.*

We are hewers of wood. And drawers of water.

*He laughs. A ringing bell from the church on the hill.*

The second chime! I will stake the team down by the brook. Won't hurt the willows. We'll come back soon as church is out and finish up. Look at him go! That boy got a cast-iron back.

*The ladle from Juny. Juny returns to work.*

You still keep a trout in the well?

**EV**
Eats the bugs.

**BIG JUNIOR**
How long do they last?

**EV**
The bugs?

**BIG JUNIOR**
The trout. You put a trout in there, how lo-o-n-g, does it last?

**EV**
Till I get hungry.

*They laugh. Maud laughs when Junior claps Ev on the back.*
*Juny picks the moss from his good shirt.*
**MAUD**
Good for you, Juny. Help your neighbours get the wood in.

*She pats him on his arm.*
**EV**
Good for the boy to learn to work.

**BIG JUNIOR**
If any should not work, then neither shall they eat.

**EVERETT**
Who you been talking to?

*Junior a calming presence.*

**BIG JUNIOR**
Everett, now. We're your neighbours. Thick or thin.

> *Junior laughs. Dad and boy turn to go.*

**MAUD**
Wait up, Junior. I got something for you.

**BIG JUNIOR**
Oh, you don't owe us nothing, Maud.

> *Maud returns with Oxen in the Winter Spruce. The board to Big Junior.*

**MAUD**
This one was Ev's idea.

> *Ev staggers. His hands to his head. Juny overlooks his father's shoulder.*

I didn't mean for you to <u>give</u> it to him.

> *Ox-bells toll. The great beasts shift in the shade. Maud sends a smile Ev's way.*

**MAUD**
Ev allus said, Junior's got the best team on the Road.

**JUNY**
Why, that's Lion. That's Bright. Look Dad. That's just the way that Lion smiles.

> *Ev squeezes in. What is all the fuss about?*

That's Bright, with the big shoulders.

> *Ev's head wobbles like a decoy on the tide.*

**EV**
The Judge would pay good cash for that.

**MAUD**
This one is Junior's. From the two of us.

**BIG JUNIOR**
Oh, no Maud. This here's your bread and butter.

**MAUD**
This one was yours. From the day Ev spoke.

*Little Juny takes the board from Dad.*

**JUNY**
Bright's short horn where he clipped the gate. You can tell that Lion is the Lead.

**EV**
Let's settle this! Well, there's the wood there. What? A cord a sticks. Then there's that picture there. Give me a dollar and we'll call it square.

**MAUD**
Go along, Junior. You more than earned it.

*Junior glances to Ev.*

He's not the boss of me.

**EV**
What?

*Maud wraps her fingers in the apron.*

**MAUD**
We'll thank you ever time we sit down by the stove.

**EV**
We got to name a price!

*A feint for the Oxen. But Ev is little match for youth and power. Juny smiles.*

**BIG JUNIOR**
We cannot serve both God and Mammon.

**JUNY**
Here we go!

**BIG JUNIOR**
We cannot serve both God and Mammon! Lay up no treasures on the earth. Where rust corrupts. Where thieves break through and steal. For where thy treasure is, thy heart be also.

*Big Junior steps up on the stump. A foot rests on the axehead.*

Yet if thy heart heed not the sound of heaven. The Lord will send the vengeance of an angel!

*Juny withdraws from Ev. Juny holds the Oxen.*

**JUNY**

Isaiah. On the subject of the lost and angels.

>*Junior steps down from the stump. He joins Juny. And addresses Maud.*

**BIG JUNIOR**

You thought enough of me and mine to give us this. This is our treasure.

**MAUD**

It's just a little thing for all you done.

**JUNY**

I shined that brass a hundred times.

**BIG JUNIOR**

Let light shine, that men may know your deeds! Juny heard this ten times in the highwood.

**JUNY**

I believe that I could give it.

**BIG JUNIOR**

Consider the lillies a the field?

**JUNY**

They toil not, neither do they spin.

**BIG JUNIOR**

Yet, Solomon, in all his glory.

**JUNY**

Was not arrayed as one a these. Dad wants me to go. To the Truro Bible School.

**EV**

They'll stop you at the limits outside town.

>*To Big Junior.*

**MAUD**

He don't mean it.

**BIG JUNIOR**

Everett. You got a tongue. Ought to be hung.

*Can't shake the anger.*

You was locked up as a child in the Poor Farm. Everybody on the Road here knows it. And your crime, and the crime of your poor mother Mary was, was, you was poor.

*A touch to the cheek of Juny.*

Who's to know? I got my hopes. I'm a man. I do take care to love my child.

*To Ev.*

Your problem. You went back there to the worst day of your life. And you stayed there. You don't sleep at night. You walk those stairs. And now the Poor Farm's shut and done. Don't you think you might need neighbours?

*Turns to Maud.*

I do apologize.

*He knows that he has sinned. He turns to Ev.*

Juny cut up every stick to fit your stove.The thing about that wood. It's dead. It's dry. You could burn it all right now.

*To Maud*

*We'll be back. And penitent. We got to stop and get Pearline.*

**MAUD**
My best to your Pearline.

**BIG JUNIOR**
She'll be standing on th'step and wondering where we are.

*Maud nudges Everett, hopefully to kindness. Ev raises a hand. Junior waits.*

**EV**
Was Pearline going to send us down another loaf?

*Not what Junior had expected.*

**BIG JUNIOR**
Man cannot live by bread alone.

*Ev wonders what the dickens this is supposed to mean. Ev thinks. And hesitates.*

**EV**
I mean a loaf of bread.

*Juny holds up the picture and whispers to Maud.*

**JUNY**
Thank you, Mrs. Lewis. We'll tack it up in the kitchen.

*Ev does not like the whisper.*

**MAUD**
You're welcome dear. We'll see yah.

*A sigh. She pats his hands. With a wave to the hill, Junior and Juny gather up their coats. Maud waves from the door and enters the House. Junior and Juny off and away. Ev is alone.*

**BIG JUNIOR**
You understand what happened there?

*Juny laughs.*

**JUNY**
Not too much!

**BIG JUNIOR**
Hush. That man back there.

*Ev picks a splinter from a finger.*

He's not all there. And he's standing with us in the passing world. But he ain't there. And then you got to try to understand.

*They turn to look at Ev. Ev picks up Juny's wood. His eyes espy the crackers on the windowsill. How to hold the wood and get the crackers?*

**JUNY**
I see.

**BIG JUNIOR**
What do you see? There's a man he's stealing crumbs from sparrows.

*Ev attempts to nick the crumbs into a pocket. He drops a stick against the door.*

You don't see that too often.

*Juny shakes his head in agreement. Maud looks out the window.*

Who the best man that you ever knew?

**JUNY**
You Dad.

**BIG JUNIOR**
I wist I was.

*Maud opens the door. Ev picks up sticks and to the House.*

**JUNY**
Uncle Bump.

*Big Junior nods.*

**BIG JUNIOR**
That's the man. Solid through. He sized it up. Stand up, or walk away.

**JUNY**
But Uncle Bumper went to jail.

**BIG JUNIOR**
He stood up. And when a man stands up, it leaves it easier for the next man comes along. That blasphemer earned what Bump give to him.

*Juny nods.*

**JUNY**
Uncle Bump sent this belt for Christmas.

*Big Junior nods. A kind caress to Juny's head. They turn to exit, Juny with the picture of the oxen.*

*To dark. Rolling thunder. Like lightning, Lion and Bright. And words from the dark of time.*

**THE VOICE OF JUNY**
Man shall not live by bread alone. But by the Word of God.

## ACT TWO SCENE TWO

# LITTLE JUNY IN THE EVENING LIGHT

*Ice cream. Bowls and spoons. The table. Maud pushes, with her knuckles, the cardboard pack.*

**MAUD**
Go ahead.

*Ev and spoon clean out the pack.*

**EV**
I never liked Vah-Nillah. Chonklit was my favourite.

**MAUD**
I'm partial to vanilla. When I was just a girl, that's all there was. You had to grate it raw. The Indies ships came in the harbour. I used to watch them coming in from out my bedroom window.

**EV**
Now! They got the three kinds. All together. Chonklit, Vah-Nilla and.

**MAUD**
Strawberry.

*He nods.*

**EV**
Here, you take it. The rest is all Vah-Nilla. I got sick one time on extract. Lord, I was ill.

*He tucks his spoon in the pocket of his shirt. She gleans the last of the ice cream.*
**MAUD**

You know what would be good? One of those old ice boxes.

**EV**
We ain't got money to buy us ice. Ice!

*He whispers.*

Melts.

You got a man coming round with a block on tongs and his bare hand out on Wednesdays. Hand me down my hand-me-down shoes.

> *Maud passes a pair of shoes, one black, one brown from the shelf. Salvage.*

I'm putting these laces in my winter boots.

**MAUD**
The butter would last. I bet Bert Potter could.

> *She doesn't dare complete.*

Everybody's getting those refrigerators. We could have had that dead red hen for dinner.

**EV**
Well it went bad that sunny day. I wasn't going to eat it anyways.

> *Maud wonders why.*

Something wicked killed that hen.

**MAUD**
Hah!
> *She laughs at her secret.*

**EV**
I gave it to the dog.

**MAUD**
I <u>thought</u> that he looked funny.

> *Ev fetches a ball of string. Maud finds scissors in a tin and places them on the table.*

**EV**
The way the winter is shaping up. We'll need ever last red cent.

> *Maud hands him scissors. Ev cuts the string for his shoes. The string to his shoes. The laces to boots.*

**MAUD**
I just thought. We had a real good summer.

> *A squeak. A rattle.*

**EV**
What was that?

*Glances to the window.*

**MAUD**
I didn't hear a thing.

*The dog barks from out back. Ev whispers.*
**EV**
See! He heard it too! Some fox is at the chickens. She got the rabbits.
Back now for the hens. Shush, she'll hear us.

*A lamp turned low. He slips on his black and brown shoes. The
Poor Farm flashlight from the shelf. He grabs a poker. To the
door.
Betrayed by shoes, he slips and turns. The light darts to the
corners.
He hangs on to the handle and slowly rises. Maud advances to
assist.*

Sh-sh-sss-h.

*A cautionary glance. Ev yanks the door and leaps into the Night.*

Juny!

*Ev can't believe it.*

I almost split your skull.

*Ev appears with Juny by the arm. Juny carefully disengages.*

I almost split his skull. I nearly. Split your skull!

*Maud turns up the lamp. Juny steadies Ev, and calmly takes the
poker. He places it aside.*
I nearly.

**MAUD**
Stop saying that! Sit down, Little Juny.

*Ev points at Juny.*

Good of you to visit. Sit by the stove.

*A chair from the corner. Juny sits at the table.*

**JUNY**
I was just passing by.

*Maud smiles.*

**MAUD**
And who were you out courting?

**EV**
Your Mum done sent you down here with a loaf of bread. You ate it.

*Ev takes the spoon out of his shirt pocket. He licks it.*

**MAUD**
Would you like a cup of cocoa? I'll heat up some Carnation.

*A glance to Everett.*

Half and Half.

*Maud grinds the cocoa with a spoon. Carnation Evaporated to a pot.*

**EV**
I amost split your skull.

**JUNY**
No, you didn't.

*Everett attempts to decipher.*

**EV**
Just where were you heading? Down to the Beach? Hooking lobsters out the rocks. Where did you hide the jute bag? How many did you get?

*Ev threatens Juny with the spoon.*

**JUNY**
I wouldn't do that.

*Ev considers Juny's rejoinder.*

**EV**
Down where the dead low tide leaves pools along the flats. What was you using for a gaff?

**MAUD**

Ev! He never said that he was down there at the Beach.

*Juny laughs. Maud serves the cocoa.*

**JUNY**

I will say, I done it in the past.

*An embrace of a smile. He taps his forehead.*

I got an idea now. I got an idea in my head. I'm on the straight and narrow.

**MAUD**

Do you take sugar?

**JUNY**

Yes, please. Mrs. Lewis.

*Everett watches Juny.*

**MAUD**

I remember when we were kids. When we came in, what we used to like was cocoa when the sun went down. And I allus liked a spoon of sugar. My brother, he liked honey.

*Juny wonders at Maud's hands.*

**EV**

Dump in the whole bowl.

*From Maud, a glint of propriety.*

**MAUD**

We have company.

*Maud speaks to Juny. She holds up her hands.*

They just look bad. It's not catching. When Ev first thought to ask, he asked my cousin Kathleen was it catching.

**EV**

It wasn't catching.

**MAUD**

Then we were married.

**JUNY**

I wonder what those hands a yours can do. Dad says, look at her. What she can do. Look what she does. Crippled and all, there's nothing stopping her.

*Maud kneads her knuckles within her apron.*

**MAUD**
I got my hard days. Just like everyone. There's lots worse off than me. There's days it's hard to get a picture done. I used to do the one or two most every day.

*Ev points with the spoon.*

**EV**
How come? You never got no mud there on your boots?

**MAUD**
Ev. If you keep on this way, he won't feel welcome.

*The spoon to pocket.*

**EV**
What was you out to get?

*Juny ignores Everett. He turns to Maud. The gesture of an open hand to the door.*

**JUNY**
I like the cranes that you put on the door. I like that. I never saw a black crane.

**MAUD**
Those cranes, they started out as swans.

*She smiles.*

**JUNY**
Black swans.

*Maud agrees.*

**MAUD**
This is the first you ever came to visit on your own.

**EV**
Far as we know.

*They size each other up.*

Walking about in the pitch black dark.

**MAUD**
Ev.

*Ev will not take the warning. Juny sips the cocoa.*

**EV**
You don't rattle on like your Dad, do yah?

*To Maud.*

I'm just telling him, for his own good, he should watch out.

**JUNY**
My Dad agrees with you.

*Ev is cautious.*
**EV**
What.

**JUNY**
He says there's people. I should be more careful with.

*Everett considers. He nods.*
**MAUD**
Let Juny drink his cocoa.

*Juny stands to look at the Sign.*
**JUNY**
Paintings for Sale. I like that too. Red robins and spring blossoms.

**MAUD**
That's just the Sign. I had to paint it. Ev had me sitting out there by the road.
The first year I was here, I was a billboard.

*They share a laugh. Juny leans in to share a confidence.*
**EV**
Well. We sold a lot.

**JUNY**
Lion. And Bright. I got it on the wall up in my bedroom. I asked my Mum. And Dad said fine with him. So I hung that one you did of Lion. And Bright. By a ribbon on my bedroom wall.

*Maud nods.*

I decided. Not to drive a nail in it. I fixed a ribbon on the back. It deserve it. I look at it all the time. I begin to see just how you did it.

*Ev leans to listen.*

**MAUD**
It's nothing.

**EV**
Once you get the board.

**JUNY**
Well. Good evening, then.

*The mug to the table. He turns to Ev.*

I share books with my cousin Mandy. That's our first cousin, Amanda Cromwell. Aunt Sandra's daughter. We order the one book of ever one. Tonight. It's her turn for the book we got a test.

**MAUD**
Oh! That was a kind kind errand.

*He turns to Maud.*
**JUNY**

I saw your light was on and hoped to stop. And say how much I liked the picture. And the way you paint.

**MAUD**
Stop again when you can stay a little longer.

**JUNY**
I hope to say I will. I got an idea what, I want to do.

*A cautious glance to Ev. Juny out the door with a parting smile.*
**EV**
Did you see that?

**MAUD**
That what?

**EV**
That look. There's more to him than he lets on.

**MAUD**
Well yes. There is. He's wondering what he's going to do. Maybe there's not a whole lot here for him. Maybe he got to go to make his way.

**EV**
You do what you got to.

**MAUD**

He's wondering what he <u>wants</u> to do.

*She knows the difference.*

He's growing up. But he's the same good child he was when he was young.

**EV**

Built like a bull.

**MAUD**

Little Juny? I guess then. You ought to stop your swinging pokers.

*She hopes the joke will temper Everett. The more he thinks about it, though, the more he grows afraid.*

**EV**

When Junior brought the wood down and the lead turn to go home, Junior lost them. "Catch hold!" And Juny took a hold a Lion by the horns and turned him in. I never saw <u>a man</u> do that.

**MAUD**

He's Pearline's boy.

**EV**

He wasn't down there on the beach.

**MAUD**

He never said he was.

*Ev mumbles.*

**EV**

He <u>never</u> come rate in the house. And then, next thing you know, why there he is.

*He points to where Little Juny sat at his table.*

**MAUD**

We never asked him in. Come and go with Pearline, don't you remember? I remember Juny round his mother's skirts, him looking in the door.

**EV**

Was he. Even then. All they wants ar money.

**MAUD**

If there's one thing we don't have. It's money.

*Ev thinks about this. He moves to bar the door and shut the*
*House down for the night.*

**EV**
Well then. What do <u>you</u> figure he was up to?

**MAUD**
Well. I don't know. Well yes, I think I do.

> *Ev halts.*

I believe. He wants to see the inside.

He's only ever been out on the outside.

> *Ev considers this, but suspicion weighs. Should she tell him*
> *everything?*

I'll tell you. The last time that Pearline was here.

> *Interrupting.*

**EV**
When!

**MAUD**
When she brought down the bread!

> *Exasperation.*

Pearline was here. She said, she said to Juny, you have been a rascal
and it didn't work. Now what are you going to do! And Juny said, to
his mother, I will become an angel. Which made his mother laugh.

> *Ev absorbs the story. He mutters but we can't hear what he*
> *says.*

I wish him well.

> *Her apron on a nail in her corner.*

*I* don't think he wants to be a minister at all.

> *Ev prepares the stove for the night. The firebox and irons. Maud*
> *removes her slippers, the slippers under the stove.*

**EV**
So much for Old Jehovah.

*He speaks up.*

Hot water bottle?

> *Maud shakes her head. She takes a coverlet from a rack, and covers her shoulders. Ev helps Maud to climb the stairs. It's a long haul.*

**MAUD**
I thank you.

**EV**
There. Good. I'll check the chicken coop. See if we still got chickens.

> *He points to the door. Ev listens at the bottom of the stairs. He turns to open and shut the door. He tiptoes up the stairs to listen. Silence.*

> *The regulator counts the hours. He descends to the Black Cabinet. He extracts a carpenter's box. Wood, tin, old, clasp, hasp and lock. He sighs.*

> *Ev glances to the attic, turns up the wick, and in the brighter light he fishes the wallet from his overalls. With a key from the top of the Cabinet, he unlocks the box. He sets aside the trays and shifts them to the table. He lifts, with reverence, a paper tied with string.*

> *Little knots. Teeth and nails. He parts the paper to disclose an inner pack of oilcloth. And from the cloth, a block of soiled cash.*

> *He separates the packs of bills. He wipes saliva from his lip with the frayed cuff of his shirt.*

> *As in solitaire, he arranges the bills in rows. Silver dollars in a stack. One last bundle is tied with a rubber band. He strips the band, takes the day's take and adds it to the bundle. He hears, or thinks he hears, a noise outside. He stands to peer around the blinds of the corner window.*

> *And finally he sneaks back to the stairs. He whispers to the loft.*

Maud. Maud. Are you sleeping?

> *Retraces steps to return the cash to the lockbox. All to their resting places. The snaps of locks.*

*He turns the chair to face the door. He sits in the dark, the iron poker in his hands. The spits and flashes of the firebox behind.*

*To Leadbelly and the dark: Irene, Goodnight. That worn and difficult to chord twelve string Stella guitar*

## ACT TWO SCENE THREE

# JUNY AND INCARNADINE

*Morning. Ev is out the door with a basket on his arm. He stops on the steps to tie the flaps of his hunting cap beneath his chin. The basket on the handle of the bicycle. He wheels out of the yard.*

*Juny enters in a patched black suit and a clean white shirt. He watches Ev depart. He takes his cloth cap off and brushes it against his pants. The cap to a pocket. He brushes his hair with his hand. He stops in the yard to take the string off a butcher-paper parcel. He knocks on the door. Maud peeks out the window. Juny holds up a loaf of bread. She cracks the door.*

**MAUD**
Juny Boy!

**JUNY**
Mum sent this down.

**MAUD**
Your Mum bakes the best bread. Is she coming by?

**JUNY**
Today is her day at the Nevilles.

**MAUD**
Well, you tell Pearline that I said she's the best. Would you like to come on in?
> *Juny hesitates.*

I was painting bluebirds.

> *From the millwheel step to the inside. Bread to a tin, and a smile for thanks.*

That's a fine white shirt that you got on.

**JUNY**
Mum said that I should wear it, before I outgrowed it.

> *The windowblind. The sun comes in.*

**MAUD**
It won't be long before it's Christmas. The frost has touched so much already.

*Juny inspects the tray. He picks up a tube of oils.*

Did you ever try your hand at painting?

**JUNY**
In school, we had crayons. We never had. In. Car. Na-deen.

*He puts it back.*

**MAUD**
That's red. Roses and hearts. These are oil paints. Some dear. Bert Potter, Bless Her Soul, she brought me these. I used to do a lot of pictures out a the scrape a cans. There's houses here to Boston with my old boat paints on their pictures.

*A blue.*

**JUNY**
How do you say this colour.

*Maud wonders at the word.*

**MAUD**
I never tried! I just go by the colours on the caps.

**JUNY**
One year my sister stole all my crayons.

**MAUD**
She never.

*A nod insists.*

**JUNY**
She took all my crayons out. She sharpened up the ends of hers and put them in my pack. I went to colour. Not much left!

*Holds up his thumb and finger.*

**MAUD**
That was Gaye?

**JUNY**
Yes. That was Gaye.

*Maud enjoys this family story.*

But I forgive her. She thought that she'd be teased without new crayons.

*Maud turns the picture on the tray.*

How long will this one take you? He picks up the board.

**MAUD**
The time just flies. I'd spend all the time on it I could. This is meant to be, a nest of bluebirds. This is the father. This is the mother. The children are inside the House. We'll leave this all white. For snow. New fallen snow, they stayed too long! They didn't want to go, and so, they got themselves snowed under.

**JUNY**
I hope they make it.

**MAUD**
And then they got to fly to where they stay the winter. We do not know.

*She sits to paint. Quick, pecking strokes.*
**JUNY**
Do you. Do you have a story every time?

**MAUD**
I guess them up. I just don't tell.

*Juny smiles. Maud points to a chair. He shifts the chair, drops his cap on a finial and sits.*

**JUNY**
What's the end of the story?

*She stops but does not answer. And then.*
**MAUD**
I just like to think they're going on and on. While I'm painting, they're just going on. They stayed to sing us one last song. Maybe a wish to see our Christmas.

**JUNY**
What were they like?

*Maud places a No. 4 flat in front of Juny. He looks at it but he does not dare to pick it up.*

**MAUD**
Everyone laid down their troubles. Out strolling. Every house a song
and doors were open.

> *A trifle embarrassed, she turns to instruction. She hides her
> hands in her apron. She drops the brush and takes an aspirin
> tablet from her pocket. She sips from a handy glass.*

**MAUD**
It's just a crick. I got to rest. But you try, Juny.

> *He picks up the No. 4. She kneads her hands.*

A little goes a long, long way.
If you edge the wing in black. It stands out.

> *She adjusts the brush. It works.*

What colour should we give his eye?

**JUNY**
Gold.

> *She substitutes a round. The brushes, scallop shells, tins and
> paints before them.*

**MAUD**
Gold is red and yellow.

> *He picks up a touch of red and yellow. Paint to the board.*

You can mix the paints rate on the board.

> *Tentative.*

A bluebird with a golden eye!

> *Pleasure in the very thought.*

Who'd a thought, and here they are. You know what I learnt about
mistakes?

> *Juny smiles.*

There's no such thing.

> *He thinks about this. He likes the idea.*

**JUNY**
Someone tell that one to Dad. He got a list.

*They share the joke.*

**MAUD**
Her eye. Gold. Yellow and a touch of red.

*Whisper.*

Try all of them. You'd be surprised the colours you can find.

*This is fun.*

**JUNY**
It's hard to get both eyes the same.

*He stops.*

My Uncle Bump was born with one dark eye.

**MAUD**
Ev speaks a Nelson. That rusty span your uncle lend a hand, to drag
the house to here.

**JUNY**
Well, I always liked him.

**MAUD**
And so you should.

**JUNY**
I'd like to do one, of Lion.

**MAUD**
Well, let's finish off the bluebirds. Then, I think. You pretty much can
do just what you like.

*The idea pleases.*

With Lion you got all the harness. It's hard. But, if you like it, that's
the secret.

**JUNY**
I been doing everything. I bin picking apples. Loading boats. We got a
share in the Brindley Weir. We'll see. How much are these?

*He holds up the brush.*

**MAUD**
Every time I look, they get more dear.

**JUNY**
I can always earn a living.

**MAUD**
I don't even like to sell them. If I had my way, I'd hand my pictures out!

*They laugh.*

**JUNY**
This wing is looking crooked. Oh. Crooked. My bluebirds are going to end up walking south.

*They smile. He paints. He picks up colours on the tip and edge.*

**MAUD**
Perfect. Look.

*She takes the brush. A correction. Juny is anxious to get the brush back.*

You got the eye.

**JUNY**
This bluebird is looking more like a swallow. Belong in a barn. I like him anyways.

**MAUD**
When the people come on by, they'll like him too. In this business, you're twice blessed. You don't need to hold the brush the way I do.

*Her hands.*

I got this as a child. I kept hoping. Some day I'd wake up. And it would be gone. But every day it got a little worse. I was so embarrassed. So I hid.

*She kneads her hands.*
**JUNY**
Hid.

**MAUD**

For years. I hid. Left school and hid. I came home and just hid out.
At the end I only had the one friend left.

*A pause in his work to listen.*

And then my mother passed away. And I come up the shore to here
to live with my Aunt Ida. I saw a notice in the paper. A woman for her
keep.

**JUNY**

Who started you on painting?

**MAUD**

It was our Mum. We used to paint these little cards, at Christmas.
Mum and I. Four for a quarter. And the money rolled in.

*Perhaps this was a joke Maud shared with her mother. Juny
paints. He begins to hum Abide with Me. He sings.*

**JUNY**

Abide with me, fast falls the eventide.
The darkness deepens. Lord, with me abide.
When other helpers, fail and comforts flee.
Help of the helpless, O, abide with me.
I fear no foe, with you at hand to bless.
Fear has no weight, and tears no bitterness.
Where is death's sting? Where, grave, thy victory?
I triumph still, if Thou abide with me.

**MAUD**

You tell your mother. A young man with a voice like that, she's got a
treasure.

**JUNY**

Oh, she knows.

*A sudden sighting.*

**MAUD**

Juny Boy, you got to go.

*Taps window. He looks out.*

**JUNY**

I guess so.

**MAUD**

Oh! You got paint on your clean white shirt.

*He buttons up his coat.*

**JUNY**

Mum won't see it under my coat.

*She scrubs the spots with her apron.*

**MAUD**

She will when you take your coat off. Take these, Juny.

*Two bristle brushes in the paper from the bread. He hesitates. The brushes to a pocket and a push. Cap to his head. He's out the door.*

*Ev, ragged as Old November, rattles in. The bicycle to the side of the House. Maud greets him at the millwheel stone.*

**EV**

Was that Junior's Juny?

*A bicycle clip. The empty basket.*

**MAUD**

Pearline sent him down here with a loaf a raisin brown.

**EV**

Looked like he was skulking.

*Maud shakes her head. Into the House.*

**MAUD**

No, no.

**EV**

Hobnobbin! Don't know what's worse, the skulkin or hobnobbin.

**MAUD**

Now, now. She could sell that bread.

*He hefts the bread.*

**EV**

Her bread's got too much airholes.

*Hooks the basket to a peg. An old and weary man. He rests.*

All that haul for nothing. They cleaned up everything. We got to stretch out what we got. The boots and laces. When Juny brings the bread, don't let him in he'll eat us out a house and home.

**MAUD**
They thought enough of us.

> *Ev cuts across.*

**EV**
No. I'm sayin no. Pearline. I'll grant you Junior got a good one. Cook and keep the house and earn a dollar on the side. When she goes to town they pay her just to watch the baby! That other evening they was here. That's the first you spoke a your brother Charles since he stole all the money.

> *Wounds hurt.*

And stuck you with your old Aunt Ida.

> *He nods and waits for Maud to nod.*

You can't trust anyone. When I'm out, that door is closed. Including Juny. What I'm sayin is, is no.

> *He nods twice. He points at the half-done board.*

What. In the name of all that's good and holy. Is that.

**MAUD**
It's bluebirds.

**EV**
Looks like swallows.

> *She looks at the board and laughs. She fetches Ev a mug of tea from the stove. He nods in desperate acceptance. Great sighs.*

Only a dummy. Ah. Would ever buy that. Ah. Ah.

> *Maud's good nature survives the criticism.*

**MAUD**
Fine. Then. I tell you what. This one we'll keep.

> *She props it up on the warming oven. To dark. Bluebirds Digging Out Their Nest.*

This one we'll keep.

## ACT TWO SCENE FOUR

# EV AND BERT TANGLE

*Exterior, evening. Ev with the bicycle to the shed out back. He locks up the bicycle. The dog barks.*

**EV**
Nothing for you.

*Interior. Maud cleans her brushes in a tin. Ev returns. The sound of brakes and motor from the Road. Ev hides behind the Cabinet. Bert peeks in the window. She raps and enters with the custom boards.*

**BERT**
Maud, Maud, it's me!

**MAUD**
And you're welcome.

*Ev sneaks a peek.*

**BERT**
I brought the boards.

**MAUD**
They're perfect. And. They're. Square!

*Ev peeks out.*

That's pretty quick.

*Boards to Maud.*

**BERT**
What's the point of a man got a mill. Lest you can tell him what to do.

*Ev shifts.*

You ought to have a fire on.

*The chickens cackle.*

**MAUD**
We had a fire early on.

**BERT**
I'll get Keith to bring some ends.

**MAUD**
Junior brought two cord but. We got to make it last.

**BERT**
Don't worry. I'll look in.

*A little hug.*

Here's a little bonus on the old brown dog.

*A black purse off her shoulder.*

**MAUD**
What?

*Maud fears Ev will soon explode.*

**BERT**
I sold that dog we cut out a the wall.

*Bert offers the five.*

**MAUD**
On no Bert, you paid for Bill.

*Maud holds the boards. Ev rockets past the Cabinet.*

**EV**
I heard you coming like you owned the road!

**BERT**
Good evening Everett. I thought that might be you back there. Back there with the hens.

**EV**
What's that!

**BERT**
Five dollars. Legal tender.

*The five to Maud.*

**MAUD**
No Bert. Can't lose a friend for a few little dollars.

*Maud returns to five to Bert. Ev's eyeballs follow the transaction.*

**EV**
You're the one that cuts the holes! Trespass. Thie-very of goods.

**MAUD**
Now Everett.

**BERT**
You have some trouble with the notion of a payment? I paid the asking price.

*Ev grows confused.*

**EV**
What's the price of a man's house? Hah? You're careful not to come on by when I'm around. You been careful there. You got no call to come between a man and.

*Sharp glance to Maud.*

His House!

**BERT**
You name the going price. Just reimburse the ten and I'll be gone.

*Ev is stumped. He trembles in frustration. The five becomes obsession. Bert waves it.*

**EV**
Listen you. Bill was my dog. You took him.

**BERT**
Then, I guess, I'll put this five away.

*She waves it to his face. Ev grabs the five. Bert gasps.*

**EV**
I'm slowed down some. But I'm still too quick for you.

**BERT**
Keep it. You bozo. And get a fire on.

*Ev folds it to a one-inch square.*

Maud, I'm sending down the girl with the iron tonic.

**EV**
I ain't paying.

**BERT**
Nobody's asking you to pay.

> *He advances. To the door? Bert shifts her purse to her shoulder.*
> *John L. Sullivan. Ev clenches his fists, but he dares not raise*
> *them.*

Come on then Bucko. Come on.

> *Ev weighs his chances.His decision is no fisticuffs. Bert*
> *straightens her shoulders.*

I thought as much.

> *Maud steps in.*

**MAUD**
We thank you Bert. For your thoughtful gift. I can paint the whole
darn lot. And Ev can sell them. One by one. We need the money.

**BERT**
You're welcome, Maud. Lovey, you best just look out for yourself.

> *A wave to Maud and to the door.*

**MAUD**
Hello to Keith! And thank him for the paints!

> *Maud tightens her apron about her waist. Bert pauses at the*
> *door, admires the swans and exits. Ev hauls on the chain to his*
> *wallet.*

**EV**
I guess I drove her off.

**MAUD**
I guess you did.

> *A bitter moment.*

I don't know where I'd be. Without her.

> *The truck backfires. Ev ducks. Embarrassed by his cowardice, he*
> *steals a glance. Ev to the fire. Coals and kindling. Maud settles*
> *into her corner. Ev brings a shawl.*

**MAUD**
She kept her word.

**EV**
She thinks a lot a The All Mighty Dollar.

*A thought.*

I'll shop at the co-op from now on. I'd like to know how much I spend. At Potters. So much a year and each year on. It must add up.

**MAUD**
You can't add.

*Weary of the struggle against self.*

**EV**
Why bother! They just take it. It all adds up to nothing.

*Maud rests. Ev selects a cardboard panel from the woodbox. He sits at the table to cut two soles for his leaky boots. Maud divides Bert's boards into two sets. Ev gets up to examine the boards.*

These are good boards. Are you feeling well enough to work?

*No answer. He returns to cut a cardboard sole.*

I wouldn't buy the iron tonic. Not from her. Why we got to pay to her to live? Not if Death Himself was knocking on the windows.

*Maud rises. The Bluebirds from the warming oven. Ev tries a sole. Satisfied.*

These are just about the last boots from the War. When they're gone, they're gone.

*Ev is vexed she does not answer. The Bluebirds to her windowsill.*

Maybe the Judge would buy those birds.

*Maud's reply cannot be heard.*

**MAUD**
I never got. To even keep the one.

*A hand behind his ear.*

**EV**
What's that.

**MAUD**
That board goes out the door, then I'll be next.

*Barely audible.*

That board goes out the door, I'll die.

*To dark. A whisp of So Long, It's Been Good to Know You.*

## ACT TWO SCENE FIVE

# THE REMEDY

*Maud completes partition of Bert's boards.*

**MAUD**
There.
> *She slowly takes a breath. Ev surveys His Wife and House.*

**EV**
I suppose you're all upset.

**MAUD**
I'm just tired.
> *She rubs her hands. Everett espies the pain.*

**EV**
You got a aspirin?
> *He searches his pockets. The tin is missing.*

Oh yes.
> *He unlocks the cabinet. The aspirin. A teacup of warm water from the kettle. To Maud. She smiles. Rain on the roof.*

Rain starting. Some morning, look out, snow on the roof.
> *They listen.*
> *He locks up the cabinet.*

**MAUD**
Here it comes. A hard rain.
> *Ev places a Scotian Gold tin on the floor.*

**EV**
Watch this.
> *They wait. Raindrops patter on the pan. Ev raises his eyebrows and smiles to Maud.*

Same every year.

**MAUD**
It gives me hope.

**EV**
It gives me the shivers.

**MAUD**
When you are good. Everett. When you are good.

> *A tremor. A trouble holding the teacup of warm water. She dabs up the drops that fall. Trouble with the aspirin going down.*

**EV**
I'd best make a fire.

> *He sets to kindling and the sticks of apple. He turns to Maud.*

I don't know. Tell you the truth. I just don't know.

> *He retreats.*

I try to think but it don't work out. Oh well.

Here we go winter. Dug the beets. The frost don't hurt a carrot.

> *He taps the stovepipe. He turns the draft.*

Got to get the smoke on up the chimney.

**MAUD**
The pipe is cold. The pipe just needs to warm a bit.

**EV**
Yes. I could make you a cup of tea. And break out some a that winter cheese.

**MAUD**
Got to tell you I'm not feeling all that good.

**EV**
What's that?

**MAUD**
It's been coming on a day or two.

> *Surprise.*

**EV**
But you was sick last week!

> *She nods.*

One time I knew that I was dying.

*He takes the trembling cup.*

Take a sip.

*She sips.*

I had a crawl start in the chest. Couldn't shake it. I tried everything.
Including kerosene.
*He taps his chest.*

Could not draw a breath. Ears went deaf. Took to bed with a blanket
and nobody come for days. Days. Nights. I missed my rounds.

*Maud wraps her shawl. Ev assists.*

Olive sent the Master by with pork rinds. Still in my bed.

*He points to the loft.*

He fired up the range and fried up all that rind. Right here. I poured
it down. I went to work that evening and I ain't dead yet.

> *Maud does not respond. Ev peers into her face. He throws three
> sticks of birch into the firebox. He thumps the sticks and coals
> with the poker. The bark roars up the chimney. He dims the table
> lamp and turns up the lamp in Maud's corner. Maud does not
> respond.*

**EV**
What can I git yah?

**MAUD**
I'm not hungry. I'm just cold.

> *Ev is seized by an inspiration. He places his coat on the back of
> her chair. He turns the chair and places her feet up and into the
> oven. She smiles. She coughs. Maud and Ev, together, smile.*

**MAUD**
That feels good.

**EV**
I could make a cup of tea with milk and sugar.

**MAUD**
Maybe.

**EV**
I remember, one time, Bill went through the ice. The pup was set to go downriver. When I caught on the collar. Good piece a leather. The last bit made that hinge.

> *Nods to cupboard.*

I carried him here. And. I lifeted him right up into this oven.

> *A searching glance. Feels the warmth of the oven with a hand.*

And he come out and lived well, oh, another, oh. What? But that was before you come.

**MAUD**
I remember. Bill was my favourite too.

**EV**
Was you here then?

**MAUD**
I remember. You carried him home in a jute bag. And Bill got better.

**EV**
Was you here then?

> *She looks away as she remembers. The rain lightens. Ev notices. And in the silence turns to Maud.*

**MAUD**
I painted Bill.

> *She is distraught. Ev does not remember.*

I was here.
> *He exhales in relief.*

**EV**
Bill. No matter what I did to him. He loved me. <u>That</u> shows you who they likes.

> *A smile.*
> *He tucks the coat about her shoulders.*

How are yah doin now?

**MAUD**

Better?

*He nods. She rests. A slow thrumming as she tries to clear her throat.*

Those boards that Bert brought down.

**EV**

You want them?

**MAUD**

No. I split'em in two packets.

*She reconsiders. She tries to breathe. He adjusts a coverlet about her legs.*

**EV**

Well, when you're ready then, sing out.

**MAUD**

I'll tell you what to do. About those boards.

**EV**

There. Bake it out. Things ar turned ar way. This year the Potters work for us. We'll never spend another silver dime. Long as we live. Oh yas. We got a good long ways to go.

*Ev places Bluebirds front and centre on the warming oven. He hopes she notices.*

There ain't they nice.

*Ev sits with Maud. A quiet wait. He stands. The batteries from wax paper and the warming oven. The radio. They enjoy the tune. He shifts the Bluebirds closer. Maud reaches out to pat his hands. He stares at Maud's hands. To dark and a fragment of Leadbelly. Light flashes on the Bluebirds.*

# ACT TWO SCENE SIX

# THE LAST ONE THAT SHE DONE

*The light is Black and White. The Judge, crowned by a hat with a black satin ribbon, discovers an old cake tin and shakes out dust. Bert enters through the ragged field of Poor Farm graves.*

**BERT**
You can't be too hard. Can't condemn them to their history. They were men. I say that in the kindest way. Go to the Poor Farm graveyard. A child was just a number on a cross. They locked up women. The whole third floor. The only job Ev ever had was locking up the women.

*She buttons up her winter coat. She takes no notice of the Judge.*

The Poor Farm. The Master Jink. The Sheriff Mutt. The Judge of the everlasting county. They had their hand in everything.

**THE JUDGE**
Those visitors from the Boston States. They retraced their steps. They hit the horn, as tourists do, and Ev went out. They did not get the greeting they expected.

*Ev in a second delineated light.*

Late in the year Maud was ill. And nothing a-tall to sell. They said.

*The Judge calls out the tourists' lines but does not look at Ev.*

This isn't fall. It's winter.

**EV**
You got a lot to learn. That last day you was here. That was the last day she was well. I got a mind to call the ambulance.

**THE JUDGE**
Our visitors took to their whispers. They saw Maud's illness as a chance to salvage something from their tour of the autumn colours. And it shocked Everett.
The offer. Forty dollars for the last one that she done. Forty Dollars.

**EV**
Wait here.

*Juny enters into the Black and White. He stands apart.*
*Ev to the warming oven of the stove. The Bluebirds.*

**THE JUDGE**
Ev creeped in. Maud watched him steal the precious thing. Bluebirds
Digging Out Their Nest.

**JUNY**
Half mine.

*He stands apart.*

**BERT**
He knew his price.

**THE JUDGE**
Ev signed MAUD LEWIS. Bottom right.

*Our ghosts now listen to each other. They do not argue, but*
*their memories are their own. The Judge shrugs to the audience.*
*Junior enters and confides to all.*

**JUNIOR**
He copied all her letters off the Sign. Paintings for Sale.

*Ev struggles with his letters.*

**BERT**
He sold it for a sum. It cost him everything.

**THE JUDGE**
There are things that I can't tell you. On account of who I am.

**JUNY**
He did not do a good job on the letters.

*The Judge, as Tourist, turns to Ev.*

**THE JUDGE**
That's not a likely S.

*Ev holds the Bluebirds out.*

**EV**
Best I can do. Short notice.

**JUNIOR**

*Bert peers in the window.*

Cold hard cash.

**JUNY**

He wrote her name.

**EV**

The name was mine before she come.

**BERT**

The story of the cash went round. The cash and what he did. And there was rumours of a lockbox in the loft. All she done and all he sold and all that. Money.

**JUNIOR**

I spoke too freely. I spoke too quick. And Juny, God Rest His Soul. He listened.

*The Judge twists the silver ring. A tear begins a long descent.*

**THE JUDGE**

It was the last one that she did before she.

*Juny is calm.*

**JUNY**

Died. She died.

*Angry.*

She died with nothing. She died with. Nothing.

*Maud rises from the stove and tries to make her way upstairs. The railing. Balance. She returns to the chair by the stove.*

*To dark. A flash of narrow light. Everett holds up Bluebirds Digging Out Their Nest.*

*Fade to dark.*

## ACT TWO SCENE SEVEN

# THE FINEST ROSES IN THE COUNTY

*Morning. Maud awakens to a dream of loss. She looks up to the warming oven.*

*Ev wipes grit off the stove with a whisk. The kettle.*

**MAUD**
The Bluebirds is gone.

*Ev lies.*

**EV**
I would have woked you up, but you was sleeping.

*Silence. She looks to Everett for the truth.*

**MAUD**
Everett.

**EV**
That's why I get those boards. That's why you paint them.

*She shakes her head.*

**MAUD**
That one wasn't ours to sell.

*Still and quiet.*

**EV**
What?

**MAUD**
That one wasn't ours to sell.

**EV**
I know you're sick.

*She listens to him lie.*

I'm looking after things.

*She grits her teeth. She looks away.*

We're going to need that money.

**MAUD**
Everything we need is here.

*Exhausted.*

I'm not going to get through this.

*A motor. It passes on the road. Ev listens to the motor pass.*

**EV**
If it's that important, you can paint another one.

**MAUD**
No.

*A motor approaches and stops. Ev is instantly alert .*

**EV**
Who's that?

**MAUD**
I don't know.

*Ev slips his feet into his boots. He walks to the window blinds and sneaks a peek. A quick knock. Someone tries the latch. Ev panics.*

**EV**
It's the Judge.

*Ev is vexed. Maud attempts to rise, then grips the blanket. As if close purchase could cover disability. The latch rattles.*

**MAUD**
The Judge.

*Maud worries for the look of her hair.*

**EV**

Spruce up. Where are your shoes?

**MAUD**
I don't know.

*Ev looks about.*

**EV**

What kind of a grown woman. Don't know where her shoes are at.

*The Judge pokes his head past the door. He enters with a Gladstone and a stringbag of oranges.*

**THE JUDGE**
Called out on a minor matter. Don't get up.

*Ev takes the oranges.*

**EV**
What big ones.

*The Judge addresses Maud.*

**THE JUDGE**
Don't get up. We'll make a fire. Do you have a juicer?

**EV**
We got a mangle.

*The Judge leans in to comfort Maud.*

**THE JUDGE**
I heard you had a touch of grippe.

**MAUD**
I bin better, Judge. It's good to see you.

*The Judge surveys the wood and Maud & Ev.*

**THE JUDGE**
We have, the all of us, seen better days. We'll get through the winter and we'll soon join hands with spring. Junior bring the wood? Good, good. I was picking up my bread and Pearline said that Junior said that Maud was down with something.

**EV**
She wasn't took sick then.

**THE JUDGE**
In point of fact, it was Junior's Pearline's boy.

**EV**
Oh. That little midnight tip-toe.

*The Judge: A flat package from the leather case. String and butcher paper bound.*

**THE JUDGE**
Word gets around.

*Maud smiles.*

**MAUD**
And a good thing too.

*To Maud.*

**THE JUDGE**
Don't be angry with me.

*She laughs.*

I brought you something.

*He cuts the string with a jack-knife. The papers parted. A production. The revelation leads to wonder. The Three Black Cats in glass and frame. The Cats to a peg on the wall.*

Rosina thought these kittens might cheer you up.

**MAUD**
I never saw one in a frame.

*She wonders at the work.*

**EV**
But we got rid of that!

**MAUD**
Judge. You don't have to listen to this. Please thank Rosina for her kindness.

**THE JUDGE**
Oh, I'll bring her out when you are better. And she will tell you just how much your kindness means.

*The Judge cleans a place on the table. He sets his satin-ribboned Homburg carefully aside. And dandily takes off his overcoat to roll his cuffs.*

And would you like a fresh Seville? The orange of English marmalade.

**EV**
He wants to know if you want one a these.

*Ev: an orange to her face.*

**MAUD**
I'm not deaf. I'm sick. Everett, please help me up.

**EV**
A course. A course.

*The Judge examines the dish. He cuts the orange in slices.*

**THE JUDGE**
Has MacCleave been out?

*Ev stops his assistance. And then panics.*

**EV**
O No Judge. I seen her worse than this.

*The Judge gestures to the road and neighbours.*
*He addresses Maud and Ev.*

**THE JUDGE**
You might want to cross and make a call. If MacCleave is out on calls, call Doctor Douglas.

*Snaps the knife.*

You got good neighbours. And tell the Doc I said to send the bill to me.

*Ev mumbles.*

It's your decision. Free advice is worth what you pay. But I'd have him out.

*Ev grumbles.*

**MAUD**
Judge. I'm sorry you seen me looking like this.

*The Judge assists Maud to a chair at the table. The Judge polishes his silver ring with a cuff. He begins to reassemble his attire.*

**THE JUDGE**

Never you mind a-tall. I was pleased to buy the picture of the little rabbit dog.

**EV**

You got Bill!

*The Judge smiles. A thought strikes.*

**THE JUDGE**

But what's it painted on?

*Neither Maud nor Ev reply.*

No matter. It's splendid as it is. And in the future.

*A minor lecture. That long judicial finger.*

I'll buy direct.

*He relents.*

Maud, dear. I'll bring your rose a little company. "When true hearts are withered and fond ones are flown, O who could inhabit this bleak world alone." I'm bringing you the finest roses in the County. Crimson and pale. You know a rose will blossom well into the winter. Where did I get those roses?

*He can't remember. He wipes his hands on his handkerchief.*

Oh yes. That farmhouse on the Old Post Road. Well. I must be going. I bought a house for taxes. The works of them was standing in the empty kitchen. Looked like trapped rabbits.

*A twist of the head in sympathy. He adds up what he has to do.*

First there's the deed. And then I got to send Mutt to evict. And then I got to get them to the Poor Farm it's a busy day.

*He sighs.*

The law's the law.

*He thinks about it. It's a burden.*

One for the Poor Men's. One for the Women's. I guess the children get the Women's Ward. I never thought about it. Safe in the Women's. I imagine. That's the third floor, ain't it, Ev?

> *Ev nods.*

So long, it's been good to know you, but I got to be getting along.

> *He repeats in song. A sigh.*

**MAUD**
I'm grateful, Judge. Your Honour.

> *The Judge straightens the Cats.*

Looks good.

**THE JUDGE**
It does, doesn't it? When you're better then.

> *The Judge nods. Maud nods. The Judge and Maud: a four-handed handshake. Smiles. Everett selects an orange.*

> *The Judge dons the black hat and knocks and rocks it all along his head. A hollow sound, like a rapping on a coconut. A grand vaudeville gesture and he's out the door.*

> *Ev eats through the rind of an orange. He feels a tooth. He exits to the woodpile, spitting seeds.*

> *Ev listens. The departure of the great black Chrysler. The sound of the V-8 engine.*

> *Maud struggles to her corner. She sits. A balance touch to the windowsill. Her hands about the boundaries of a board. It's a darn good board.*

> *She hides one packet of Bert's boards behind her chair. The rest are left to view. She looks to Everett out the window. Ev spits a seed.*

> *To dark.*

# ACT TWO SCENE EIGHT

# THE BOOK OF ACTS

*The evening fades. Ox bells from afar give voice. The dusk obscures our characters. We see their goods by the light of a window and a lantern.*

*Little Juny enters the yard, Big Junior a step behind. Junior carries a pot with a swinging wooden handle. Junior passes Juny with a tug on the elbow.*

*Ev is at the chopping block. Ev turns to Junior. And then returns to the axe and stump.*

**JUNIOR**
Hello there Ev-rit.

*The lack of a salutation.*

We came along. To see if there was anything that we could do.

**EV**
Don't need a preacher. We just had the lawyer. Next thing you know, the doctor's walking in.

*Juny reveals a partridge on a string. He hangs it on the nail that once held Paintings for Sale. Junior places the stewpot on the step. A hand on Ev's shoulder. Ev twists away and lodges the axe in the stump. He turns to face his visitors.*

**JUNY**
We would like your Maud to know we're thinking of her.

*Ev hesitates.*
**EV**
Lest I'm mistaken, that's what prayers is for.

*Junior takes the harm. Juny takes the pot from his father and steps up. Junior seizes the wrist of his son. Juny ought to go no further.*

**JUNIOR**
The Missus sent this over. She says to heat it up real slow. It's a chowder.

**EV**
I believe. I know how to heat a chowder.

*Juny: the stewpot to the door.*

**EV**
Hey! Git out, you little spook.

*Ev throws a looping, weak right. Or maybe the onslaught is just a grab and push. Juny takes it calmly on the back of the head. He holds the pot up and away so it won't spill. Junior grabs Ev's hands. Juny keeps his calm.*

**JUNY**
I set it down.

*Juny sets the pot on the step. He steps back.*

**JUNIOR**
No call for that. When Juny saw that Maud was sick. He got upset.

**EV**
Nobody goes in-side. Unless I say.

*Silence.*

**JUNIOR**
Now, Ev.

**EV**
I'm on to him. Well there's no money here!

*Junior places Ev's hands together. He shakes them in a settlement and lets them go.*

**JUNIOR**
We're not out for the money.

*Junior lifts the pot to Ev's hands.*

We don't want your money. The Bible says that money never dies, but only leads to death. We're just trying to get by on the least we can.

**JUNY**
Hear that.

*Juny might intend, "I hear that." Or possibly "You better listen."*

**EV**
From here on in, when I go out, they'll be a shotgun fixed to that front door.

**JUNY**
The only door you got.

*A glance to silence Juny.*

**JUNIOR**
Now, now Ev. No call to get so short with Juny.

*A breath, and his best to bring peace.*

Juny knocked that fool hen out of a crab apple tree. With the buckle of his belt. Said he would bring it down to you.

*Juny picks the partridge off the House. He holds it out but Ev won't move.*

**JUNY**
I wrung its neck.

*Junior takes a cautious breath.*

**JUNIOR**
If Pearline sent him down with just one loaf a bread, it's been a hundred. And ever you said one word of thanks, nobody can't recall.

*But Ev cannot give thanks.*

Juny thinks a good good deal of Maud. Should it come, no tellin.

*Junior hesitates. It's a battle to retain what he has studied.*

What kind of a place this would be. The Lord moves in mysterious ways. You can't dispute it. Accept it. And I am asking you to take our prayers. Accept. What little that we got to offer.

*Juny holds the partridge to Ev's chest. Juny drops it. Ev catches it.*

**EV**
That's the thinnest, bone rake bird I ever seen.

**JUNY**
You're welcome.

*Junior raises a hand to shush his son. To Juny this is useless: This man ought to be tossed in the harbour. That's what Uncle Bump would do.*

Come along Dad.

*The son lends a hand to the father. Ev dismisses Junior with a wave. Junior speaks to Ev's back.*

**JUNIOR**
You know where we live.

*Juny hears his father plead. He doesn't like it.*

**JUNY**
Come along, come along, Daddy.
*Juny and Junior walk away. Ev calls.*

**EV**
Junior!
*Junior halts and turns.*

**JUNIOR**
Ev?
*Junior waits for a thankful word.*

**EV**
She want the pot back?

*Little Juny laughs at the ignorance. Words collide in the sharpest of air.*

**JUNIOR**
What!

**EV**
Gone Judah! Does your woman. Want the pot.

*Shocked silent, Junior gapes. Juny advances to slaughter Everett where he stands. Junior reaches to grab his son.*

**JUNIOR**
No!

*Dad and Boy. Each other's arms. At first in anger. Then for comfort. Junior struggles to take Little Juny off. They rest.*

Your Uncle Bump drug this house down here. With Lion's mother. It come to pass. The prophet is ashamed, a his vision.

**JUNY**
What.

**JUNIOR**
What are these wounds in my hands?

**JUNY**
Yes. Those with which I was wounded, in the house of my friends.

> *Junior pats his boy on the back. Juny holds his father as they depart.*

**JUNIOR**
That's the one.

> *Ev watches the travelling light. A musical phrase, a single, singing gospel bell. The notes of a melody: "Lord with me abide."*
>
> *Ev picks up the partridge and lays it out on the block. He wants to knock its head off with the axe. The axehead sticks in the wooden block. He can't get it out.*

**EV**
Nice evening.

> *Confusion with the partridge, pot and door. Ev enters the House. A light on the axe. To dark. The melody. Out of the darkness.*

**THE VOICE OF JUNIOR**
The Lord will send an Angel.

## ACT TWO SCENE NINE

# ASK A LAST FAVOUR

*Maud stands by the Cats. The weary Ev. Trouble standing. He rests. Pearline's pot to the back of the stove. The partridge to a nail. He cleans the drops of blood.*

**EV**
That was Junior.

**MAUD**
Yes.

**EV**
You still sick.

**MAUD**
Yes. I'm afraid. I'm afraid so.

**EV**
The fire's out. You got to tend it.

*And then he apologizes.*

A fire and a sleep. You'll be all right.

*He watches her every breath.*

What are you doing?

*No answer.*

What do you want?

**MAUD**
I want to sit in my corner.

**EV**
It's over here.

*He points.*

**MAUD**
I want the Cats.

*He understands. He assists her to the corner. The Cats so Maud can see it to the corner. He watches her as he walks about. He stops. She settles in.*

**EV**
You want your paints?

**MAUD**
Not right now.

*A coverlet.*

**EV**
There. How are you feeling then.

**MAUD**
Not so good.

**EV**
Are you hungry?

*Nil.*

Are you cold?

*Nil.*

I can heat you up a bowl a chowder.

*He waits.*

Pearline made it. Junior brought it down.

*Their names as currency.*

**MAUD**
I am cold.

*Ev weighs her reply. Birchbark and birch to the firebox. He stops to stare. He puts on the kettle. Something further escapes her lips.*

**EV**
What did you say?

**MAUD**
A drink of water.

**EV**
Sure, sure.

> *At the reservoir of the range.*

**MAUD**
From the brook.

**EV**
From the brook?

**MAUD**
I want a drink of water from the running brook.

> *He waits. He wonders why.*

**EV**
I can heat you up a cup a tea.

**MAUD**
I don't want to die. Without a drink a water from the brook.

> *Ev stares, and then exits with the pail. She sits and rocks. Ev returns. The water to the reservoir. A trickle to a glass. He offers. She sips.*

**MAUD**
Ev.

> *She sips.*

**EV**
Yes.

> *He takes off his coat and cap.*

**MAUD**
I'm asking you.

**EV**
A course.

**MAUD**
His Wife.

**EV**
His wife?

**MAUD**
Me, Ev. Me. I want. You. To have them cut. His Wife.

*He doesn't understand.*

Into the stone.

*Fear. He tucks her coat around her.*

**EV**
You rest.

**MAUD**
His Wife.

*A step in one direction. A step in another. What to do. Then quick to the Cabinet. The key and the lock and the box. A copper noose of silver rings aside. A glance to Maud. A hand of cash and out and to the Road.*

*To Black and White and the passing past. Bert enters from the Road.*

**BERT**
Into the past. Take care where you might tread. Even a footfall can summon a ghost. The mixture. The precious cure. And Ev went out. Too late. Too late for anything. Too late for everything. Too late. You think that you escape but you are only dead.

*As Bert speaks, Junior wanders to a grave.*

Ev come to the store. The cash down on the counter. Then home to Maud and laden with the hope of life.

*Junior is unknown and unheard.*

She painted all the county, from the Waldec Line to Mavillette, man and beast and all our labours. You be prepared, if you should choose to walk into an empty room and wonder at a painting on a white lathe wall. It looks so simple. You'd be wrong. It does take time. But time, is given.

*In the yard a sharp and narrow light. From the darkness, Juny to the block. He jerks the axe, effortless, out of the block. Into the House. Ev is alone and locking up the cabinet. Juny swings the lockbox from Ev. Juny shakes the coin and cash into the firebox. A struggle but Ev is no match for the man. Ev against the open oven door. Juny strikes the flat of the axe once against the open oven door.*

**JUNY**
Hear that ring?

> *The ring fades. Light to Juny's face alone. To darkness. Lights out on Juny. Lights up and Junior in a gathering of ghosts.*

**JUNIOR**
Maud was buried in a child's coffin. Ev had the letters cut "Maud Dowley" on the stone. Maud went first. Pneumonia and starvation.

**BERT**
Ev was murdered on a New Year's Day. He didn't get too far into the year. Maud Dowley was her maiden name. Ev had it cut upon the stone. Maud Dowley. Wife, but not His Wife. She had a Dowley child. Ev knew it. Ev knew everything. Would not forgive her even when she died.

> *Junior takes a pocket Bible from his pocket. He unzips it.*

**JUNIOR**
Ev was survived by the empty lockbox in the House. The little dog down, he killed her, the day before he died.

> *Junior shakes his head.*

Whether the money was, for Ev, or Maud, is not for you or I to even guess.

> *Junior notices that the light grows stronger.*

**BERT**
You can't say Maud, the dear thing, a tragedy. She did better than most everyone.

And when he lost his job. What are we going to live on? The answer is: The love of those who love you. There was wealth. He could not see it.

Was our story, same as what she painted. All living on the same one road.

She died from a tumble down the stairs. Ambulance. A little stay, and she came home to die. But that's what did her in, she never quite recovered. Skin and bone. She didn't get enough to eat.

The day that Maud was buried, a rainbow came above St. Mary's

Bay. That evening when the sun went down, the clouds were pink like blossoms.

## JUNIOR
What my boy done I can't condone. But that. Has little enough to do with love.

We miss our son. I cannot tell you just how much. He trusted yah. He loved yah. Each day brings new remembrance. Up to his room and look at his things. His books, that pork-pie hat he wore out on the docks, the picture that Maud Lewis done a Lion.

Some day some child take up his destiny, I'll watch him work and hear him sing, it will be like our Juny has come back. Little more wonderful, when a child that you don't know, says hello. We miss our son.

*The Light brighter on Bert. Junior twists in the dim. The church bells, the regulator, and the strike of an axe on iron.*

## BERT
The Judge got old, his vices clustered. He lost the great collection of her pictures. That deep cathedral against the gathering dark. For a hand a money. Greed got him.

He bought a mansion on the shore. Up the street from where his mother worked the trade and he as a boy slept in an attic room, he and his brothers above the busline station, the little in the middle.

The Judge died. At the last, he thought he was a Lord.

The poor a the county went on as before, and one, that Dime Trefry, who dug the odd grave, on account of his aunt, the bootlegger, what the Judge had put in jail, buried, for eternity, the Judge there upside down.

Pearline's boy. His Uncle Bumper found him, by the meadow. Below the Ridge where the brook cuts in the meadow on the gravel shoal. Beneath old elms. His arms held, like so, his hands together. Grim and determined he would not be caught. His skin dull silver, a thin rime a ice. The ground was frozen. His Uncle Bumper got two men and carried him home. Bumper took him home and broke the news.

*Lights out on Bert.*

**JUNIOR**

Keith and Bert Potter, good people, gone. Good neighbours, they're all gone. Don't think too poorly a the Judge he was only flesh and blood.

The Poor Farm. Ever day Jink opens up the door. Before I die, the ground in which those innocents lie buried will be blessed. They'll have them more than numbers on a cross. Mark my words. It is the flowers, in the night, bring that to pass.

*A study at the Bible.*

**JUNY**

I went to the Judge. I told him what I done. And he said Juny Boy, you got to run for it. Don't go home. Don't talk to anyone. So I cut across the country and I stayed off the roads. I got so tired. And I just laid down for a rest. I didn't make it.

**JUNIOR**

And when you think of her, some time you are alone, say this to silence. Keep on lost soul. Learn to do well. Recall the questing heart of Nathanael. Recall the answer.

Seek judgement and plead for the widow. Relieve the oppressed. Esteem the orphan cast aside. Help the child is motherless. If we believe in this, then victory.

*The Bible folded in his hands. The Bible into his pocket. The cross to view.*

Maud Lewis. The best and most famous of our County. To this day, I wonder. Was it love?

*Lights out on Junior.*

*Maud appears. To the storm door with a brush. Bright light to Maud. She freshens up the heart on the door. All the hidden colours flood. Maud confides to the audience. She is now a ghost and speaking to a great confederation.*

**MAUD**

That first day we were married. We drove the Model T along the river. The brook was up and came right over the road. The Model T kept stopping on the hills. I had to get rate out and walk I didn't mind. Those trees and leaves above the road Up on the Ridge. Down Acacia Valley.

*Lights dim on Bert and Junior, Juny and the Judge. They stand together as at a funeral. They watch to the end.*

The first thing I got done. I hooked a big rug for the floor. The House sat on the ground. And Bert stopped by and bought the rug. That's why the two of us wore slippers.

And if the years were not as great as those first days. There were summer days you couldn't trade for anything. The idea that it pleases some to hang my pictures in their kitchens is something. That is something.

It wasn't easy. I made my mistakes. I still harbour my regrets. I thought. I'll do my best and the day will come when I can make amends. Mostly, I only want what everyone wants. I want to be forgiven.

> *Into the House. The door is open. Everett returns with the greenglass bottle. Colours seep into the Black and White.*

> *Ev into the House. The rocker is still. Maud is still. He holds up the greenglass bottle so that she can see.*

**EV**
You'll be better soon. You will. Soon. A warm, warm fire and a rest. Maud dear, are you sleeping?

> *Ev, kindly, nearly touching, sets the rocking chair to its slight rocking. The chair runs down to still.*

> *Ev places his arm around Maud, as if to assist her to rise. He sits beside and stares. He places his hand to his mouth. He leans to embrace. In fear he withdraws. A racking cry escapes. A gasp from his chest.*

> *One by one, like dominoes, lights out on Bert and Junior and the Judge and Juny.*

> *Church bells and ox bells. To dark. The long toll.*

> *Paintings for Sale in a lightning flash. Thunder.*

> *Wilf Carter: a fragment of There's a Bluebird on Your Windowsill.*

## The End

*Barton, Digby County, Nova Scotia*
*April, 2016*

Maud Lewis World Without Shadows

Made in the USA
Middletown, DE
15 December 2017